Luigi Pirandello

THREE MAJOR PLAYS

A Smith and Kraus Book
Published by Smith and Kraus, Inc.
177 Lyme Road, Hanover, NH 03755
www.smithkraus.com

First Edition: December 2000
10 9 8 7 6 5 4 3 2 1

Cover and Text Design by Julia Hill Gignoux, Freedom Hill Design
Cover Illustration: Starry Night Over the Rhone *by Vincent Van Gogh, 1888*

The Library of Congress Cataloging-In-Publication Data
Pirandello, Luigi, 1867–1936.
[Selections. English. 2000]
Luigi Pirandello : three major plays / Luigi Pirandello ; translated by Carl R. Mueller.
p. cm. — (Great translations series)
Includes bibliographical references.
Contents: Right you are (if you think you are) ; Six characters in search of an author ; Henry IV.
ISBN 1-57525-231-7
1. Pirandello, Luigi, 1867–1936 — Translations into English. I. Mueller, Carl Richard. II. Title.
III. Great translations for actors series.

PQ4835.I7 A274 2000
852'.912—dc21   00-049681

Luigi Pirandello

THREE MAJOR PLAYS

Translated by Carl R. Mueller

Great Translations Series

SK
A Smith and Kraus Book

FOR MY MOTHER

Contents

Introduction

The position of Luigi Pirandello (1867–1936) in the history of the modern theater is about as secure as it is possible to be. He is without question the greatest Italian playwright of the twentieth century, and one of a select handful of international playwrights of the same distinction. Almost singlehandedly in the years following the First World War, he waged his own war against the general tenor of the theater of his time: naturalism. In doing so he liberated the stage, transforming it from a platform on which people "acted" rôles— pretending they were the people they "acted," and pretending that the fake parlors in which they "acted" those rôles were real. Pirandello, whose work in the theater (as well as in his novels and stories) is based solidly on the assumption that reality is an unknowable factor, disagreed with the conceit that the stage was a site for "real" events to unfold in "real" terms. In play after play he undermined it to the best of his ability, which, as his body of work testifies, was considerable. Willing suspension of disbelief was not for him. The side of beef in the butcher's window on the stage of André Antoine's Théâtre Libre in Paris in the 1880s may have been the real thing, but the window was not the window of a real shop, and the people in the scene were not the real people who would inhabit such a shop. And so, troubled by such pretense, Pirandello created a theater that eschewed the raw, undigested material of naturalism and put in its place a central concern with abstract thought and philosophical commentary on the foibles of being human.

But Pirandello was a man of the theater and not an armchair, or even a professional, philosopher. He knew that his theater, in addition to being a place for philosophical rumination, had to be a place for adventure and delight. We too often look at Bertolt Brecht as the inveterate, humorless thinker in the modern theater—the one who energetically sacrifices entertainment for serious thought, the "intellectual" playwright. This is as unfortunate as it is unenlightened, for Brecht's theater is built on the premise of "sweetness and light," of enjoyment and illumination. If there is a single word that describes the basic aesthetic of Brecht's theater, it is laughter. No one who has seen Brecht's productions of his own plays in the former great days of the Berliner Ensemble can say otherwise. The same is true of Pirandello, with one major difference: Pirandello's theatrical laughter is of a different sort;

it is ironic in a way that Brecht's is not. And that irony is the tool that Pirandello uses to make his point.

In one of Pirandello's greatest and most endurable plays, *Right You Are (If You Think You Are)*, the ringmaster in the circus of illusion and reality that identifies that play is named Laudisi. He subtly guides the action (albeit from a quite distanced emotional remove), taunting, probing, questioning (always with tongue-in-cheek, I-told-you-so irony). Finally he arranges a culminating confrontation that will pull the plug on the mistaken assumption that truth is ascertainable.

A mother-in law and her (former?) son-in-law and his wife move to the capital of an Italian province. The wrinkle is that they live apart; that the mother-in-law believes the wife is her daughter; that the son-in-law refuses to allow the mother to enter her daughter's apartment, as well as disallowing his wife (whoever she is) to leave it. This causes mother and "daughter" to "visit" at a distance, between an upper-story tenement balcony and the courtyard far below by means of written messages exchanged in a basket that is lowered and raised between them.

This arrangement very soon becomes the talk of the town. How can this boorish son-in-law refuse visiting rights to this poor mother? And the town arranges a cabal to investigate the matter. Separately, first the mother-in-law's story is told, then the son-in-law's. The problem is that each story contradicts the other, and the son-in-law's story casts doubt on the sanity of the mother-in-law. At the end of this brilliant first act another appearance by the mother-in-law casts doubt on the sanity of the son-in-law, and at the same time makes very clear that the mother-in-law is merely playing a humanitarian rôle to help the son-in-law in his distraught mental condition over the death of her daughter (his wife) in an earthquake. Inch by inch the rug of truth is pulled out from under the "citizen investigators," as well as out from under the feet of the audience. In the end, when a confrontation is arranged between the mother-in-law, the son-in-law, and the daughter/wife, we learn that there is no truth, that the mother-in-law's "truth" is right for her, that the son-in-law's "truth" is right for him, and that the daughter's "truth" is right for her. Truth, therefore, is not a given; but rather, it is determined by each person's individual need. Truth is a totally subjective reality, which is to say: an illusion. Ibsen would have called it a "life-lie."

An intellectual playwright? Yes. But with a difference. For all the headiness and intellectual baggage of his philosophical stance Pirandello is equally (and perhaps foremost) a total man of the theater. His characters are never mouthpieces—political, ethical, aesthetic, or otherwise. They are vivid, they are immediate; they are, unequivocally, "more" than life. In a word, they are "theatrical" creations whose *raison d'être* is to take part in a platform presentation of an idea. These characters cannot be separated from the play's theme because they exist only for that theme and for the fable that contains them. They are eminently "real" because they are, in fact, not real. And that is Pirandello's triumph. And that is, perhaps, his greatest and most lasting contribution to the modern theater: theater as "theater," theater as "play," and theater as "game." That is to say, theater whose intent is to make the mind reel in the ironic laying on of ambiguity and uncertainty.

Though he began writing plays in 1910, Pirandello found his mature "voice" as a playwright in 1917 with the writing of *Right You Are (If You Think You Are)*. The First World War drawing to a close and, as is usual at the end of such a cataclysmic event, the world was beginning to question some of its basic traditional moral and ethical values. Pessimism and skepticism were the result of this questioning. "Truths" once taken for granted were now being subjected to rigorous investigation. And this "investigation" is the stuff of Pirandello's art. Illusion, reality, truth, personal identity—among other issues—were there to be questioned and evaluated from a new perspective. Truth, as has been said, was impossible to know, or, perhaps even more strongly, did not, in fact, exist. Illusion must inevitably take the place of reality because reality is forever a mystery (as is truth). Identity is not categorical and is not governed by givens. Or, as one critic has said "is not intrinsic and individual, but extrinsic and multiple . . ." We—our identities—are determined by every rôle and situation that circumstance forces upon us: We are a different person for everyone we meet and different every time we meet them. Objective knowledge does not exist. This assault on truth and identity is the subject of *Right You Are (If You Think You Are)*. Pirandello the humanist argues for the acceptance of the inexact, the subjective, the ambiguous, and the anomalous that are the product of illusion. To Pirandello, life is difficult enough *with* the balm of illusion to help one survive. To be denied that balm is to invite disaster. Illusion, then, is the humanitarian alternative to having to endure and suffer the deprivations and indignities of a cruel and wretched world: It is a *sine qua non*.

It is the choice made by Henry IV in the play of the same name. A head injury—suffered twenty years ago during a historical carnival cavalcade in which he wore the costume of the German Emperor Henry IV—left him fixated on the idea that he *was* that Henry. For the eight years that follow the accident, he lives *as* Henry IV, in a villa that is outfitted in the manner of an eleventh-century castle, with servants in historical costume living out his fantasy for him (while in his presence, that is); he "rules" as the emperor. Eight years later he wakens from his fixation, and choosing not to live again in the harsh external world "as it is," he decides to continue the charade—to continue "being" Henry IV, and to continue the pretense/illusion even to his servants. But, implies Pirandello, is all this to be believed? It is not impossible even to ask oneself whether he was *ever* insane? Not to question it is, perhaps, to be intellectually lazy. But the question will never find an answer even if Henry himself gives testimony, because is *he* to be believed? This, then, is the nature of a Pirandello play.

Never the abstract, ivory-tower intellectual, Pirandello's work spills over with human warmth and sympathy for the individual whose life has been disrupted—shifted out of a quiet, ordinary daily routine whether by accident or design, and made to suffer that expulsion because life has suddenly been rendered impossible. It becomes livable again only when the expelled has built up a defense, a mask to live behind a persona. It was not incidental that Pirandello gave the umbrella title of *Naked Masks* to his collected plays.

In *Six Characters in Search of an Author,* we find ourselves in new territory, in a territory that invites comparison with German expressionism. The so-called expressionist "scream" is well known. It occurs over and over: the gaping mouth of the horse in Picasso's *Guernica,* the primal cry of the expressionist poets, the wrenching late orchestral interlude in Berg's *Wozzeck* that builds to a climax and an intensity that threatens sanity itself. They were created by the mind of an author who then decided not to use them. Their "lives" have been sidetracked by fate. They have been left floundering in their search for an author (any author) to use them as they were meant to be used: in the play the original author intended them for. As they say in the play, they have that story inside them; it merely needs to be released.

For all the play's intellectual superstructure, there is no shortage of visceral analysis of character in *Six Characters in Search of an Author. This* is self-analysis carried out not at a distance, but laceratingly by the characters themselves, with all the pain of flesh and blood characters. No academic, textbook intellectualization, no dabbling in philosophical speculation; rather, torment, pain, brutal honesty that arises out of a suffering that is the product of a ruthless displacement: from an author's mind into the oblivion of a rootless existence. The Father of the family of Characters lays out Pirandello's philosophical position with raw and unequivocal honesty:

> For me drama exists in one thing—the knowledge that each of us believes himself to be a single individual. But it's not true. Each of us is many indi-

viduals, many—each of us has many possibilities of being. We are one thing for this person, and another for that, and each of them is quite different. Yet we suffer under the illusion that we are the same person for everyone. But it's not true. Not true. We perceive this—perhaps tragically—when suddenly we find ourselves caught in mid-act. And realize that not every possibility in us was involved in that act. It would be an atrocious injustice to be judged by that act alone—to be held responsible for it throughout eternity—to be pilloried—as if all of our existence had been summed up—in that one act. Do you now understand the treachery of this girl? She surprised me in a place where she should never otherwise have met me. And in an act that I should never have been doing with her. And as a result of this one fleeting, shameful moment of my life, she presumes to read the totality of my existence. And this, *this,* is what I feel most strongly about.

All in all, Pirandello bore witness to the inconsistency of all things, and to the vain struggle of humankind to grasp the unattainable. And like his contemporary Bertolt Brecht, he provided no answers—most likely because he didn't have any. His theater has been called "the theater of mirrors," for, just as in the mirrors of an amusement park fun house, we see the world (reality) distorted into an illusion, an illusion that demonstrates the illogicality of logic, which, in the end, is the only reality.

CARL R. MUELLER
Department of Theater
School of Theater, Film, and Television
University of California, Los Angeles

Right You Are
(If You Think You Are)

(Cosi è, se ui pare)

A Parable in Three Acts
1917

CAST OF CHARACTERS

Lamberto Laudisi
Signora Frola
Signor Ponza *her son-in-law*
Signora Ponza
Counselor Agazzi
Signora Agazzi *his wife*
Dina Agazzi *their daughter*
Signora Sirelli
Signor Sirelli
The Prefect
Centuri *Police Commissioner*
Signora Cini
Signora Nenni
A Butler
Other Ladies and Gentlemen

TIME AND PLACE

The Capital of an Italian Province, 1917.

Right You Are
(If You Think You Are)

ACT ONE

Drawing room in the home of Counselor Agazzi. Main door at rear; side doors, right and left. LAMBERTO LAUDISI is a man of about forty, elegant of manner, and dressed in a violet jacket with black lapels. AMALIA AGAZZI is about forty-five, has gray hair, and displays a sense of importance derived from her husband's place in society. At the same time, she makes it plain that if free to do so she could play her own rôle in the world and perhaps even better than her husband. DINA AGAZZI, their daughter, nineteen, leaves no doubt that she understands all things better than her mama and papa, yet this defect is tempered by her youthful liveliness and charm. At rise, LAUDISI is seen pacing back and forth in irritation.

LAUDISI: Ah! So then he did go to the Prefect!

AMALIA: But, Lamberto! The man is his subordinate.

LAUDISI: In the office, perhaps. Not outside.

DINA: But he took an apartment for that woman on the same floor as ours.

LAUDISI: And why shouldn't he? The apartment was for rent. He leased it. He moved in his mother-in-law. Since when is a mother-in-law required to visit the wife and daughter of her son-in-law's superior officer?

AMALIA: Required? It was Dina and I who made the first move. She refused to receive us.

LAUDISI: And so your husband complains to the man's boss? Do you expect the law to force her to invite you to tea?

AMALIA: I expect some kind of reparation. You don't just leave two ladies standing outside a door.

LAUDISI: Haven't people the right to their own privacy?

AMALIA: But it was we who extended the courtesy. To make her feel at home.

DINA: Don't get so excited, Uncle. I'll admit. Our courtesy was more out of curiosity. But is that so terrible?

LAUDISI: Terrible? Yes. Because you have nothing to do all day.

DINA: All right now, Uncle. Let's just suppose. Here you are. Minding your own business. Very well. Then I come in. Face long as an undertaker's. Like that gentleman's you're defending. And—plop—I drop here on the table in front of you—a pair of the cook's shoes!

LAUDISI: *(Indignantly.)* What have the cook's shoes got to do with it?

DINA: *(Quickly.)* There. You see? It startles you. And you insist I explain at once.

LAUDISI: *(Momentarily taken aback, smiling coldly, then recovering himself.)* Dear, dear Dina. Such a clever girl. But I'm your old uncle, remember. So. You come in. You dump the cook's shoes on the table in front of me. And with no other reason than to incite my curiosity. Well, what am I to do but ask for an explanation? But now show me, please, how Signor Ponza installing his mother-in-law in an apartment next to yours is in any way comparable. Did he do it on purpose?

DINA: On purpose? Of course not. But he's certainly raised a lot of curiosity since coming to town. The first thing he does is rent an apartment on the top floor of a filthy old tenement on the outskirts. Have you seen it? From the inside, I mean.

LAUDISI: But *you* have, of course.

DINA: Of course. And so has Mama. And we're not the only ones. Everyone's been out to have a look. There's a courtyard. Dark as a bottomless pit. And a balcony around the top floor. With baskets hanging from it. On long strings.

LAUDISI: And . . . ?

DINA: *(With astonished amazement.)* It's where he keeps his wife!

AMALIA: While his mother-in-law lives next door to us!

LAUDISI: In a nice apartment in the center of town.

AMALIA: Yes! To keep her away from her daughter!

LAUDISI: Oh? Perhaps she prefers her freedom.

DINA: No, Uncle! You're wrong! Everybody knows it's his fault.

AMALIA: Excuse me. When a girl marries, and leaves her mother, and goes to live with her husband in another town, it's perfectly natural. But when her poor mother follows them? Because she can't live without her daughter? To a town where they're both strangers? Well, isn't it odd for her not only to have to live alone, but not even be allowed to *see* her daughter?

LAUDISI: Perhaps he doesn't get along with his mother-in-law. Is that so strange? Maybe it's his fault. Maybe hers. Or neither's! Incompatibility can . . .

DINA: *(Interrupting, in amazement.)* Oh, Uncle! If anyone's incompatible, it's mother and daughter!

LAUDISI: Why bring the daughter into it?

AMALIA: Because the other two are thick as thieves!

DINA: Mother-in-law and son-in-law! Whoever heard of such a thing?

AMALIA: He comes every evening. To keep her company.

DINA: And once or twice each day, too.

LAUDISI: Are they lovers?

DINA: Oh, please. She's a poor old lady.

AMALIA: But he never, never comes with his wife. Mother and daughter are not allowed to see each other.

LAUDISI: Perhaps she's ill, poor thing. Perhaps she can't go out.

DINA: No. The mother goes to see *her*.

AMALIA: Exactly. But only from a distance. It's a fact that she's not allowed in her daughter's apartment.

DINA: She speaks to her from the courtyard.

AMALIA: Can you imagine? The courtyard!

DINA: And the daughter looks down at her. From that balcony in the sky! The poor old lady goes into the courtyard, pulls the string attached to the basket that rings a bell, and out comes the daughter. She has to talk with her head thrown back like this. And can't even see her properly. With all the light streaming down from above!

(There is a knock at the door and the BUTLER enters.)

BUTLER. Callers, madam.

AMALIA: Who is it?

BUTLER. Signor Sirelli and his wife. And another woman.

AMALIA: Ah. Show them in.

(The BUTLER bows and goes out. SIRELLI, SIGNORA SIRELLI, and SIGNORA CINI enter. SIRELLI is a man of about forty, fat, balding, pomaded, with a pretence to elegance. SIGNORA SIRELLI, his wife, is a plump, red-haired woman who is still young; she, too, is provincially overdressed, ardent in her curiosity, and severe with her husband. SIGNORA CINI is a foolish old biddy full of malicious delight that she hides behind a façade of artless ingenuity.)

AMALIA: *(To SIGNORA SIRELLI.)* My dear Signora Sirelli!

SIGNORA SIRELLI: I took the liberty of bringing along my good friend Signora Cini. She's been dying to meet you.

AMALIA: How delightful. Make yourselves at home. *(Continuing the introductions.)* This is my daughter Dina. And my brother. Lamberto Laudisi.

SIRELLI: *(Greeting them.)* Signora. Signorina. *(He goes to shake hands with LAUDISI.)*

SIGNORA SIRELLI: My dear Signora. We come here as to the font of all knowledge. Two poor pilgrims parched with the thirst for information.

AMALIA: Information? About what?

SIGNORA SIRELLI: Why, about that blessed new secretary. At the prefecture. Signor Ponza. The whole town's talking about him.

SIGNORA CINI: We're simply devoured with curiosity.

AMALIA: But we know as little as you, Signora.

SIRELLI: *(To his wife, triumphantly.)* You see? As little as I! And maybe less! *(To the others.)* Do you know the *real* reason why this mother can't visit her own daughter's home?

AMALIA: I was just discussing that. With my brother.

LAUDISI: I think you're a pack of gossips!

DINA: *(Quickly, so as to take attention away from her uncle.)* They say, because her son-in-law forbids it.

SIGNORA CINI: *(In a wail.)* That's not all, Signorina!

SIGNORA SIRELLI: *(Emphatically.)* That's not all! There's more!

SIRELLI: *(Spreading his arms so as to garner attention to himself.)* The very latest word is that he—*(With great clarity.)* keeps her under lock and key.

AMALIA: His mother-in-law?

SIRELLI: No, Signora! His wife!

SIGNORA SIRELLI: His wife! His wife!

SIGNORA CINI: *(Wailing.)* Under lock and key!

DINA: Well, Uncle? So much for your excuses . . .

SIRELLI: *(Astonished.)* Excuses? For that monster?

LAUDISI: But I'm *not* making excuses for him! I'm saying that your curiosity . . . if the ladies will pardon me . . . is insufferable! If only because it's useless.

SIRELLI: Useless?

LAUDISI: Useless! Yes! Useless!

SIGNORA CINI: But all we want is to know!

LAUDISI: Know what, Signora? What can we know about anyone? Who they are? What they are? What they do? Why they do it?

SIGNORA SIRELLI: By picking up bits and pieces. By gathering information . . .

LAUDISI: In which case, you have the lead on all of us. Your husband being the best informed person around.

SIRELLI: *(Not unflattered.)* Oh, well, really . . .

SIGNORA SIRELLI: No, no, my dear. It's true. *(Turning to AMALIA.)* The truth is, Signora, my husband, who claims to know everything, tells me nothing worth believing.

SIRELLI: And why should I? She never believes anything I say. She begins by doubting. Then maintains it can't be so. And finally is convinced that the very opposite is true.

SIGNORA SIRELLI: Oh! You should hear some of the things he says.

LAUDISI: *(Laughs loudly.)* If I may, Signora. I'll answer your husband. *(To SIRELLI.)* How, my dear Sirelli, can you expect your wife to believe what you tell her, when what you tell her, naturally enough, is expressed from your point of view?

SIGNORA SIRELLI: Which is absolutely impossible!

LAUDISI: No, Signora. Now it's *you* who are wrong. What your husband tells you is true. As he sees it.

SIRELLI: As it is in reality! As it is in reality!

SIGNORA SIRELLI: No! You're *always* wrong!

SIRELLI: I am not always wrong! It's you who are always wrong!

LAUDISI: No, no, no! Please! Neither of you is wrong. Let me prove it. *(He walks to the center of the room.)* Now. Both of you. Look at me.—You see me, don't you?

SIRELLI: Of course!

LAUDISI: No, no. Don't be rash. Now. Come here. Come here.

SIRELLI: *(Smiles with a puzzled expression on his face, not certain he wants to take part in a joke he doesn't understand.)* Why?

SIGNORA SIRELLI: *(Pushing him, in an irritated voice.)* Go on!

LAUDISI: *(To SIRELLI, who approaches with hesitation.)* Do you see me? Look at me more closely. Touch me.

SIGNORA SIRELLI: *(To her husband, who is still hesitating.)* Touch him!

LAUDISI: *(To SIRELLI, who lifts one hand and touches him on the shoulder.)* Good! Bravo! Now. Are you certain you're touching me? As well as seeing me?

SIRELLI: I'd say so.

LAUDISI: I can see you have no doubts. You may sit down.

SIGNORA SIRELLI: *(To SIRELLI, still standing stupidly in front of LAUDISI.)* Stop standing there batting your eyes! Sit down!

LAUDISI: *(To SIGNORA SIRELLI, after her bewildered husband has returned to his seat.)* Now. Signora. If you will please. Come. Over here. *(Quickly, correcting himself.)* Or no, no! I shall come to you. *(He walks over to her and goes down on one knee.)* You see me? Don't you? Now. Lift your hand.

Touch me. *(Still seated, SIGNORA SIRELLI puts one hand on his shoulder. LAUDISI kisses it.)* What a charming hand!

SIRELLI: Easy! Easy!

LAUDISI: Ignore your husband!—You're certain that you're touching me? As well as seeing me? No doubt in your mind, then.—But now I want you to promise not to tell your husband, or my sister, or my niece, or Signora . . .

SIGNORA SIRELLI: *(Coaching.)* Cini . . .

LAUDISI: Cini . . . what you think of me. Because they would all say that you're wrong. Completely. But you're not wrong. Because I really am just as you see me. But that doesn't prevent your husband, my sister, my niece, and Signora . . .

SIGNORA SIRELLI: *(Coaching.)* Cini . . .

LAUDISI: Cini . . . also from seeing me as I really am. Each in his own way. Each of them is right.

SIGNORA SIRELLI: Then are you a different person? For each of us?

LAUDISI: Of course! A different person! Aren't you? Don't *you* change?

SIGNORA SIRELLI: *(Very quickly.)* Change?! I certainly do not! Ever!

LAUDISI: Nor I. From my standpoint, that is! Believe me! And I would say that each of you is wrong if you fail to see me as . . . I see myself. But that would be presumptuous of me. As it is of you, dear Signora.

SIRELLI: What does all this have to do with anything!

LAUDISI: What has it to do with anything? I see you people running around in circles. Trying to find out who and what everyone is. As if everyone had to be this or that and nothing else.

SIGNORA SIRELLI: Are you saying that it's impossible to know the truth?

SIGNORA CINI: I can't believe what I see and touch?

LAUDISI: Of course you can, Signora! All I'm saying is that you should respect what others see and touch. Even if it's the opposite of what you see and touch.

SIGNORA SIRELLI: I don't want to *hear* about this! I don't want to *talk* about it! It will drive me *insane!*

LAUDISI: Very well. I'm done. You may continue talking. About Signora Frola. And Signor Ponza. I won't interrupt again.

AMALIA: Thank God for that! It would be even better, Lamberto, if you left altogether.

DINA: Indeed it would, Uncle. Go! Go!

LAUDISI: No. Why should I? I enjoy hearing you talk. But I won't say another word. I promise. At most, you'll hear a laugh or two out of me. And if it's too loud, you'll just have to forgive me.

SIGNORA SIRELLI: We only came here to find out . . . Excuse me, Signora.
But isn't your husband the superior officer of this Signor Ponza?
AMALIA: At the office, Signora. At home . . . no.
SIGNORA SIRELLI: Of course.—But haven't you even tried to see the
woman? Since she's only in the next apartment?
DINA: Tried? We've tried twice, Signora!
SIGNORA CINI: *(With a bounce; then all agog.)* Ah! Well then! Then you
have talked to her!
AMALIA: We weren't allowed inside the apartment.
SIGNORA SIRELLI, SIRELLI, SIGNORA CINI: Oh! Oh! Why was that?
DINA: This very morning . . .
AMALIA: The first time we waited in front of the door more than a quarter
of an hour. No one answered. We weren't even able to leave our calling
card. So we tried again. This morning . . .
DINA: *(Throwing up her hands in a gesture of horror.)* And *he* opened the door.
SIGNORA SIRELLI: With that face of his! Horrible! No wonder everyone's
talking. And that black suit of his . . . They all dress in black. The
Signora. And her daughter . . .
SIRELLI: *(Irritated.)* But no one's ever seen the daughter! I've told you that
a thousand times! She probably wears black . . . They come from a vil-
lage in Marsica . . .
AMALIA: Yes. The one that was destroyed.
SIRELLI: Wiped out. Totally. By the last earthquake.
DINA: Along with all their relatives, I've heard.
SIGNORA CINI: *(Impatient to return to the interrupted story.)* And? So what
happened then? He opened the door . . .
AMALIA: And the minute I saw him in front of me, with that face of his, I
could hardly find the words to tell him that we'd come to visit his
mother-in-law. But there was nothing! Not even a word of thanks!
DINA: Well, he did bow.
AMALIA: A little one, I suppose. With his head. Like this.
DINA: More with his eyes, I'd say! Oh! You ought to see them! Like some
kind of animal's rather than a man's eyes!
SIGNORA CINI: *(Still impatient.)* Well? What happened then?
DINA: He was terribly embarrassed.
AMALIA: Almost angry. He said his mother-in-law wasn't feeling well. But
that our kindness was much appreciated. And then he just stood there.
Waiting for us to leave.
DINA: I was mortified!

SIRELLI: What a boor! Ah! But you can be sure! It's his fault! Perhaps he even keeps his mother-in-law under lock and key!

SIGNORA SIRELLI: The nerve of the man! And with a woman! The wife of his superior officer!

AMALIA: Yes, well. My husband really took offense at that. Lack of courtesy, he called it. He's gone to complain. To the Prefect. And demand an apology.

DINA: And here he is! Here's Papa now!

(COUNSELOR AGAZZI, a man of fifty, enters. His hair and beard are red and unkempt and he wears gold-rimmed spectacles. He is authoritarian and ill-natured.)

AGAZZI: Ah, my dear Sirelli! *(He goes over to the sofa, bows, and shakes hands with SIGNORA SIRELLI.)* Signora!

AMALIA: *(Introducing SIGNORA CINI.)* Signora Cini . . . my husband!

AGAZZI: *(Bows and shakes hands with SIGNORA CINI.)* A great pleasure! *(Then turning to his wife and daughter with some solemnity.)* I may tell you that Signora Frola will be here any minute.

SIGNORA SIRELLI: *(Clapping her hands in delight.)* Will she really? She's really coming?

AGAZZI: Of course! Could I tolerate my house and my women to be so insulted?

SIRELLI: Absolutely not. Just what we were saying.

SIGNORA SIRELLI: And it would have been quite proper to . . .

SIRELLI: *(Anticipating her.)* . . . to inform the Prefect of all the rest that people are saying about this gentlemen? Never fear. I've done so.

SIRELLI: Ah! Wonderful! Wonderful!

SIGNORA CINI: Such inexplicable behavior! Really inconceivable!

AMALIA: I never heard of such a thing! He keeps them both under lock and key.

DINA: Now, Mama! We're not certain about the mother-in-law yet.

SIGNORA SIRELLI: But we are about the wife.

SIRELLI: And the Prefect?

AGAZZI: Ah, yes. Well. He wasn't at all pleased. But very impressed with my report . . .

SIRELLI: I should hope!

AGAZZI: Some of the talk had already reached him. And . . . and he agrees this mystery needs to be cleared up. The truth laid bare.

LAUDISI: *(Laughing loudly.)* Ha-ha-ha-ha!

AMALIA: Lamberto's usual contribution. His laugh.

AGAZZI: What's there to laugh at?

SIGNORA SIRELLI: He says it's impossible to know the truth.

(The BUTLER appears in the doorway.)

BUTLER: Excuse me. Signora Frola.

SIRELLI: Ah! There she is!

AGAZZI: Now, my dear Lamberto, we'll see how impossible it is!

SIGNORA SIRELLI: Oh, wonderful! I'm so happy!

AMALIA: *(Rising.)* Shall we have her in?

AGAZZI: No, no! Sit down! Please! Wait for her to come in. Just remain seated. Remain seated. *(To the BUTLER.)* Show her in.

(The BUTLER goes out. A moment later SIGNORA FROLA enters and all rise. SIGNORA FROLA is an old lady, slight of stature, and modest and affable in nature. There is great sadness in her eyes that is mitigated by the constant gentle smile on her lips. AMALIA steps forward and takes her hand.)

AMALIA: Come in, Signora. *(Keeping hold of her hand, she makes the introductions.)* My old friend Signora Sirelli. Signora Cini. My husband. Signor Sirelli. My daughter Dina. And my brother, Lamberto Laudisi. Please. Make yourself at home, Signora.

SIGNORA FROLA: I'm so sorry. Please excuse me. I've failed in my social duty to you. *(To AMALIA.)* You, Signora, have been so very kind in honoring me with the first call. When it was for me to call on you.

AMALIA: But, Signora, we're neighbors. It's nothing. I merely thought that, being alone, you might have needed help . . .

SIGNORA FROLA: Thank you. Thank you. You're too kind . . .

SIGNORA SIRELLI: Then you *are* all alone in our town?

SIGNORA FROLA: No. I have a married daughter. She hasn't been here long either.

SIRELLI: And your son-in-law? The new secretary at the prefecture? Signor Ponza?

SIGNORA FROLA: That's right. And I do hope Counselor Agazzi will excuse me. As well as my son-in-law.

AGAZZI: To be honest, Signora, I was a bit put out . . .

SIGNORA FROLA: *(Interrupting.)* And rightly so. Rightly so! Still, I hope you forgive him. You see, we haven't yet recovered. From our misfortunes.

AMALIA: Of course! That terrible earthquake!

SIGNORA SIRELLI: You lost relatives?

SIGNORA FROLA: All of them . . . All of them, Signora. There's nothing left of it. Our little village. A pile of ruins in the countryside. Totally abandoned.

SIRELLI: Yes! We heard about it!

SIGNORA FROLA: I had only a sister. And her daughter who wasn't married. But my poor son-in-law. He was much harder hit. Lost his mother, two brothers, their wives, a sister and her husband, and two small nephews.

SIRELLI: A massacre!

SIGNORA FROLA: You don't recover from such a shock. You're never quite the same.

AMALIA: Oh, I know!

SIGNORA SIRELLI: And so suddenly! It could drive you insane!

SIGNORA FROLA: You do things without thinking. Without ever wanting to, Counselor.

AGAZZI: Please. No more of that, Signora.

AMALIA: It was in consideration of your misfortune that my daughter and I made the first move to see you.

SIGNORA SIRELLI: *(Excitedly.)* Exactly! They knew how lonely you were! Forgive me for asking, Signora. But after such a terrible disaster, and with your daughter here . . . well . . . *(Losing herself momentarily, then continuing.)* it seems to me . . . well—that, that you'd want to be together . . .

SIGNORA FROLA: *(Interrupting to spare SIGNORA SIRELLI's embarrassment.)* You're asking why I live alone . . .

SIRELLI: Yes. Well. It does seem strange. To be very honest.

SIGNORA FROLA: *(Sadly.)* I understand. *(She pauses, then continues as if searching for an escape.)* But . . . well, I, I believe that when a son or a daughter gets married, they ought to be left alone. To make their own life.

LAUDISI: Very good! Exactly! A life different from anything they've known.

SIGNORA SIRELLI: Excuse me, Laudisi! But there are limits! A daughter doesn't shut a mother out of her life!

LAUDISI: Who said anything about shutting her out? If I understand correctly, here is a mother who realizes that her daughter cannot, indeed must not, remain bound to her as in the past, since she has her own life to lead.

SIGNORA FROLA: *(With much gratitude.)* Yes, exactly, Signore! Thank you! That's just what I wanted to say.

SIGNORA CINI: But I imagine your daughter will be coming here to see you quite often . . .

SIGNORA FROLA: *(Ill at ease.)* Of course . . . yes . . . we do see each other. Certainly.

SIRELLI: *(Quickly.)* But your daughter never goes out of the house. At least no one has seen her.

SIGNORA CINI: Perhaps she has children to look after?

SIGNORA FROLA: *(Quickly.)* No. There aren't any children yet. And there probably won't be. She's been married for seven years. She has a lot to do around the house, of course.—But that's not the reason. *(She smiles sadly; then continues as if searching for an escape.)* Women who . . . who live in the country . . . aren't used to going out much.

AGAZZI: Not even to visit their mother? When their mother doesn't live with them?

AMALIA: But it's probably Signora Frola who visits her daughter.

SIGNORA FROLA: *(Quickly.)* Of course. Why not? I go once or twice a day.

SIRELLI: And do you climb all those steps? To the top floor? Once or twice a day?

SIGNORA FROLA: *(Very pale, trying to cover her pain at this interrogation with a laugh.)* Well. No. I don't go up. That's true. It's much too high for me. I don't go up. My daughter comes out onto the balcony. In the courtyard and . . . and we see each other. We talk.

SIGNORA SIRELLI: That's all? Don't you ever see each other? Up close?

DINA: *(Putting an arm around her mother's neck.)* As a daughter, I wouldn't want *my* mother climbing all those stairs. But I could never manage seeing her and talking to her from that distance. Never putting my arms around her. Never having her close to me.

SIGNORA FROLA: *(Upset and embarrassed.)* You're absolutely right. Exactly. Let me explain.—You mustn't think my daughter is something she's not. That she has no consideration or affection for me. Nor must you think such things about me. Not all the stairs in the world could prevent a mother, no matter how old and weak, from going to her daughter's side and holding her to her heart.

SIGNORA SIRELLI: *(Triumphantly.)* You see! Just what we've been saying! There must be a reason!

AMALIA: *(Pointedly.)* You see, Lamberto? A reason!

SIRELLI: *(Rapidly.)* It's your son-in-law, isn't it?

SIGNORA FROLA: Oh, please, you mustn't think badly of him. He's such a good boy. You can't imagine how kind he is to me. How affectionate.

How gentle. And then how loving and caring he is toward my daughter. I couldn't have dreamed a better husband for her.

SIGNORA SIRELLI: I see . . . well, then!

SIGNORA CINI: Then your son-in-law isn't the reason!

AGAZZI: Of course not. Can you imagine a husband forbidding his wife to visit her mother? Or preventing the mother from visiting her daughter?

SIGNORA FROLA: But no one has forbidden anything. He's forbidden us nothing. We're the ones, Counselor—my daughter and I—who deny ourselves that pleasure. Out of regard for him. For his feelings.

AGAZZI: I'm sorry. Excuse me. But how could he be offended? I don't understand.

SIGNORA FROLA: It has nothing to do with being offended, Signor Agazzi.—It's a feeling he has . . . a feeling that's . . . not easy to understand. But once you do understand, it's easy to sympathize with him. But, believe me, it's a great sacrifice for my daughter and me.

AGAZZI: You must admit, Signora, that what you've been telling us is a bit . . . unusual.

SIRELLI: Unusual enough to arouse more than a little curiosity.

AGAZZI: And, may I add, suspicion?

SIGNORA FROLA: Suspicion? Of my son-in-law? How can you say such a thing? What suspicion?

AGAZZI: That's not what I said. Don't be frightened. I merely suggested there might be.

SIGNORA FROLA: No, no! Of what? We're in perfect agreement! We're happy! All of us! Both I and my daughter! Very happy!

SIGNORA SIRELLI: Is he perhaps jealous?

SIGNORA FROLA: Jealous? Of his mother-in-law? I don't think that's possible. But of course, I can't be sure.—It's like this . . . he wants all of his wife's love for himself. Even the love she feels for me . . . which he finds quite natural. Except that this love must reach her through him. Through him alone. So there you are.

AGAZZI: You will excuse me. But I consider that outright cruelty.

SIGNORA FROLA: No, no! Not cruelty! You must never say that, Signore! Believe me. It's something entirely different. It's not easy to say . . . Nature, perhaps. No, no. That's not it . . . Perhaps it's more of an illness. A kind of excess of love. Closed in on itself. Yes. That's it. An exclusive love. That his wife must live inside of and never leave. Nor can anyone enter it.

DINA: Not even her mother?

SIRELLI: I've never heard of such selfishness!

SIGNORA FROLA: Selfishness? Perhaps. But a selfishness that gives totally of itself. To the one it loves. I would be the selfish one if I tried to intrude into that love. Into that closed world. Where I know my daughter is happy. Where I know she's adored. *(To the WOMEN.)* Shouldn't that satisfy any mother?—And after all, I do see my daughter. I talk to her . . . *(Continuing in a more confidential tone.)* There's a little basket. In the courtyard. Hanging by a string. And in it we exchange letters. With news of the day's events.—That's enough for me.—I've gotten used to it. Resigned, perhaps. I don't suffer from it anymore.

AMALIA: Well, if all of you are happy . . .

SIGNORA FROLA: *(Rising.)* Oh, yes. It's just as I've said. Believe me. He's very kind. It couldn't be better.—We all have our little failings. And we must treat each other with understanding. *(She says good-bye to AMALIA.)* Signora. *(Then to SIGNORA SIRELLI, SIGNORA CINI, and to DINA; finally she turns to SIGNOR AGAZZI.)* I hope you've forgiven me . . .

AGAZZI: Oh, Signora! What a thing to say! We're delighted with your visit.

SIGNORA FROLA: *(Bows to SIRELLI and LAUDISI, then turns to AMALIA.)* No, no! Please! Don't get up, Signora!

AMALIA: Not at all! Please! I'll show you out!

(SIGNORA FROLA goes out accompanied by AMALIA, who returns a moment later.)

SIRELLI: So there we are! Are you satisfied with the explanation?

AGAZZI: Explanation? It's a greater mystery than ever!

SIGNOR SIRELLI: Poor woman. Who knows the pain she must suffer.

DINA: Oh, and the daughter!

(Pause.)

SIGNORA CINI: *(From a corner of the room where she has gone to hide her tears.)* You could hear the tears in her voice!

AMALIA: Oh, yes! And when I mentioned climbing all those stairs! To be with her daughter!

LAUDISI: I was most impressed with her determination to protect her son-in-law.

SIGNORA SIRELLI: Why, she couldn't find a single excuse for him.

LAUDISI: Excuse? For what? Has there been violence? Brutality?

BUTLER: *(Enters; in the doorway.)* Excuse me, sir. Signor Ponza is here. He would like to see you.

SIGNORA SIRELLI: Oh! It's him!

(There is a general sense of surprise and movements of anxious curiosity that come close to revealing a fear of impending trouble.)

AGAZZI: He wants to see me?

BUTLER. Yes, Signore. That's what he said.

SIGNORA SIRELLI: Oh, please, Signor Agazzi! Let him come in!—I'm almost afraid of the man. But I'm very curious to see him up close. The monster!

AMALIA: What could he want?

AGAZZI: We shall see. Sit down, now, sit down. And you must remain seated. *(To the BUTLER.)* Show him in.

(The BUTLER bows and goes out. SIGNOR PONZA enters a few moments later. He is a short, dark, thickset man of almost threatening appearance, dressed all in black. He has black, thick hair on a low forehead, and a black moustache. He continually makes fists of his hands and speaks with a force that borders on violence. From time to time he wipes the sweat from his face with a black-edged handkerchief. When he speaks, his eyes are hard, fixed, and sinister.)

AGAZZI: Come in, Signor Ponza, do come in! *(Introducing him.)* Our new secretary, Signor Ponza—my wife—Signora Sirelli—Signora Cini—my daughter—Signor Sirelli—and my brother-in-law Laudisi. Do make yourself comfortable, won't you?

PONZA: Thank you. I'll only take a moment of your time.

AGAZZI: Would you care to talk to me in private?

PONZA: No, I can . . . I can say what I have to say in front of all of you. In fact, it's . . . it's an explanation . . . something I feel it's my duty to tell you.

AGAZZI: It has to do, I presume, with your mother-in-law calling on my wife? If that's the case then you really needn't go on, because . . .

PONZA: No . . . no, it's not that at all, Signor Agazzi. No . . . I . . . simply wanted to say that Signora Frola, my mother-in-law, would certainly have paid a visit to you long before your wife and daughter so kindly visited her, if I hadn't done everything possible to stop her. I can't, you see, allow her to make or to receive visits.

AGAZZI: *(With considerable resentment.)* And may I ask why not?

PONZA: *(Growing increasingly angry despite attempts to control himself.)* I assume that my mother-in-law has told you all about her daughter— that I will not allow her to come into my house to visit her.

AMALIA: Oh, no, not at all! Signora Frola spoke of you with the highest regard!

DINA: She said very nice things about you.

AGAZZI: And that the reason she doesn't visit your daughter's apartment has to do with certain feelings of yours . . . feelings, I must confess, that we really don't understand.

SIGNORA SIRELLI: If we were to say what we really think, however . . .

AGAZZI: Yes, well . . . we'd have to call it an act of cruelty—an act of considerable cruelty, in fact!

PONZA: Yes, and that's exactly what I've come to explain, Signore. This woman finds herself in a most pitiful condition. But no less pitiful than my own in having to come here under considerable pressure to apologize . . . to reveal to you a misfortune that I would never otherwise have revealed. (*Pause as he looks around the room at everyone, then continues slowly, stressing every syllable.*) Signora Frola is insane, mad.

ALL: (*Stunned.*) Mad?

PONZA: For four years now . . . yes.

SIGNORA SIRELLI: (*Shouting.*) But, good God, she doesn't seem mad!

AGAZZI: (*Disconcerted.*) How can she be mad?

PONZA: She may not look it, but she is. And her madness consists in believing that I won't allow her to see her daughter. (*In a spasm of terrible emotion.*) What daughter, for God's sake?! Her daughter's been dead for four years!

ALL: (*Simultaneously, astonished.*) Dead?—Oh!—But how?—Dead?

PONZA: Yes. Four years ago. It's why she went mad.

SIRELLI: But . . . but the woman you live with now . . . ?

PONZA: I married her two years ago. My second wife.

AMALIA: And Signora Frola believes that . . . your wife is her daughter?

PONZA: You might almost say that's been her salvation. One day from her window in the place where she was being treated, she happened to see me pass by with my second wife. She took it into her head that in my wife she saw her own daughter—alive. She suddenly began laughing and trembling all over. She was suddenly lifted from her black despair into this other form of madness. Exultant, carefree at first, she became gradually more calm. There were signs of distress, of course, but she found a way of resigning herself to it. In any event, she's happy now . . . as you saw for yourselves. She insists on believing that her daughter is alive and that I want to keep her all to myself and never allow her to see her again. In a way one could say she's cured. To the degree that she seems quite sane when she speaks.

AMALIA: It's true! You could never tell!

SIGNORA SIRELLI: Yes, and she actually says that she's happy this way.

PONZA: She says that to everyone. She has real affection for me. And she's grateful. She knows I try to help in any way possible. And at great personal sacrifice, I might say. I have to maintain and provide for two households. Fortunately my wife is a considerate woman. She goes along with it all. Confirming Signora Frola's illusion that she's her real daughter. She comes to the window, speaks to her, writes her little notes. But charity goes only so far. I refuse to force my wife to share a home with her. As it is, my poor wife is already a kind of prisoner, locked indoors, afraid every moment that Signora Frola will try to get into the house. The old lady is calm, of course, and a very gentle person, but you can just imagine the effect on my wife of having to accept the woman's affectionate caresses.

AMALIA: *(Horror and pity in her voice.)* Of course! The poor woman! I can just imagine!

SIGNORA SIRELLI: *(To her husband and SIGNORA CINI.)* Ah, so you see? She agrees to being locked up. Understand?

PONZA: *(Cutting the conversation short.)* You can see now, Signor Agazzi, why I couldn't allow her to call on you till I had absolutely no choice.

AGAZZI: Yes. Of course, of course. I understand perfectly now.

PONZA: Anyone with a misfortune like mine is best advised to keep to himself wherever possible. Since I was forced to allow my mother-in-law to visit you, I felt it my duty to give you some kind of explanation. Out of respect, you understand, for my office, and to keep the whole town from believing in such an absurdity. Believing that for jealousy or some other reason I would keep a poor mother from seeing her daughter. *(Rises.)* I trust you will forgive me, ladies and gentlemen, for having, however unwillingly, disturbed you. *(He bows.)* Signor Agazzi. *(He then bows in front of LAUDISI and SIRELLI.)* Gentlemen. *(Goes off through the main door.)*

AMALIA: *(Bewildered.)* Ah . . . so, then, she's mad!

SIGNORA SIRELLI: The poor thing! Mad!

DINA: And that's the reason! She believes she's her mother, and the other one isn't even her daughter! *(Hides her face in her hands in horror.)* Oh, God!

SIGNORA CINI: Who would ever have guessed!

AGAZZI: Mm . . . I wouldn't be too sure—from the way she was talking.

LAUDISI: You saw that from the start?

AGAZZI: No . . . I wouldn't say that exactly. But she did have trouble finding the right words.

SIGNORA SIRELLI: Well, of course she had trouble, poor woman! She wasn't thinking rationally!

SIRELLI: I'm sorry, but there's something rather odd here, if she really is mad. I agree. She wasn't thinking rationally. But the way she searched for reasons why her son-in-law wouldn't let her see her daughter; then manufactured excuses to justify him, and finally to adapt herself to those excuses . . .

AGAZZI: Oh, that's beautiful! That's exactly what proves she is mad! This constant search for excuses for her son-in-law, without ever finding an acceptable one.

AMALIA: That's right. Everything she said she finally retracted.

AGAZZI: *(To SIRELLI.)* Do you think that, if she weren't insane, she'd accept such conditions? To see her daughter only through a window? And for the reasons she gave? A husband's morbid love for his wife and wanting to have her all for himself?

SIRELLI: Right! And would she accept those conditions if she were mad? Would she resign herself to them? I find it all very odd, all very strange. *(To LAUDISI.)* What do you think?

LAUDISI: Me? Not a thing!

(A knock at the door; the BUTLER enters.)

BUTLER: *(Looking rather disturbed.)* Excuse me. Signora Frola has returned.

AMALIA: *(Alarmed.)* Good God, again? Aren't we ever to be rid of her?

SIGNORA SIRELLI: Yes, I understand. Now that you know she's insane!

SIGNORA CINI: Mercy me, what new story has she thought up now? I can't wait to hear!

SIRELLI: Yes, I'm curious myself. I'm not at all convinced she's mad.

DINA: There's certainly nothing to be afraid of. She's so calm.

AGAZZI: We certainly have to let her in. We'll hear what she has to say, and if need be we'll take measures. Sit down, now. Everybody. And stay there. *(To the BUTLER.)* Show her in.

(The BUTLER goes out.)

AMALIA: For heaven's sake, help me! I have no idea what to say to her now!

(SIGNORA FROLA enters. AMALIA, somewhat timidly rises and approaches her; the others look on in bewilderment.)

SIGNORA FROLA: May I?

AMALIA: Of course, Signora, of course! As you can see, my friends are still here . . .

SIGNORA FROLA: *(With an affable but extremely sad smile.)* . . . and looking at me—as are you, Signora—as a poor old madwoman. Isn't that so?

AMALIA: No, Signora, what are you saying?

SIGNORA FROLA: *(With great regret.)* Ah, better to have been rude, Signora, and let you stand outside my door, as on your first visit. How could I have known that you would return and force me into making this visit, the consequences of which I already foresaw?

AMALIA: No, not at all, you must believe me. We're delighted to see you again.

SIRELLI: The Signora seems quite distressed . . . and we don't know why. Why not let her tell us?

SIGNORA FROLA: Didn't my son-in-law leave here just a while ago?

AGAZZI: Why, yes, he did, Signora. He came to . . . to see me about certain . . . certain matters involving the office, you see.

SIGNORA FROLA: *(Wounded and dismayed.)* You're telling me that kind little lie only to ease my mind . . .

AGAZZI: Nothing of the sort, Signora. I assure you, you can believe me.

SIGNORA FROLA: *(As above.)* Was he calm, at least? Did he speak calmly?

AGAZZI: Calm? Of course. Calm as can be. Isn't that true?

(They all nod, confirming his words.)

SIGNORA FROLA: Oh, God! I know you're all trying to reassure me, and here I am trying to reassure *you* . . . about my son-in-law.

SIGNORA SIRELLI: But why, Signora? We've already told you that . . .

AGAZZI: . . . that he came to see me about office business.

SIGNORA FROLA: But I can see from the way you're looking at me! Be patient with me, please. It's not my fault! From the way you're looking at me, I know that he came to prove something that I would not have revealed for anything in the world! A while ago you were all witness to the fact that the questions you asked me—and harsh questions they were, too—well . . . I . . . I simply didn't know how to answer them. I explained about our life together in a way that couldn't possibly have satisfied anyone. And I admit that! But what could I do? Tell you the truth? No! Nor could I tell you the story *he* told you! That my daughter has been dead for four years, and that I'm a poor old madwoman who believes her daughter still lives and that her husband won't let me see her.

AGAZZI: *(Astonished at the profound sincerity of her manner.)* Yes, but what, then? Your daughter . . . ?

SIGNORA FROLA: *(Quickly, anxiously.)* So then it's true! Why are you trying to hide it from me? He told you . . .

SIRELLI: *(Hesitatingly as he studies her.)* Yes . . . in fact . . . he did say . . .

SIGNORA FROLA: I knew it! Knew he had! And I also know how difficult it must have been to be forced to say that about me! What a terrible misfortune this has been, Signor Agazzi. But we've learned to overcome it, to endure it . . . although with great effort and suffering. The only way to go on living is to continue exactly as we are. I'm well aware, of course I am, that people are beginning to notice, that scandal and suspicion are to be expected. But on the other hand, if he's a splendid employee, zealous and meticulous in his work . . . Surely you've noticed this yourself, Signore.

AGAZZI: Well, no, to be quite honest, I haven't yet had the chance.

SIGNORA FROLA: Oh, but you mustn't judge him by appearances, I beg of you! He's the very best. Every one of his employers has said so. So why torment him by prying into his family life? Into an unfortunate situation which, I repeat, has been overcome, and which, if it became known, could well compromise his career?

AGAZZI: No, Signora, you mustn't distress yourself. No one wants to torment him.

SIGNORA FROLA: How can I not suffer when I see him forced to tell this absurd, terrible story? Can you really believe that my daughter is dead? That I'm mad? That this woman is his second wife? But it has to be that way. He has to believe it. Without it he has no peace of mind. No self-confidence. But he knows what he's saying. And he knows how absurd it is. And when he's forced to tell this story, he gets all excited . . . confused. You must have seen that.

AGAZZI: Yes, in fact he . . . he was a bit excited.

SIGNORA SIRELLI: Does this mean that . . . that *he's* the one who's mad?

SIRELLI: Of course! What else could it mean? *(Triumphantly.)* Ladies and gentlemen, it's what I've said all along!

AGAZZI: Oh, but really, now! Is that possible?

(General agitation.)

SIGNORA FROLA: *(Quickly, joining her hands.)* No . . . no, no, you mustn't think that! This is the one thing that he can never have mentioned to him. Can you believe I would leave a daughter of mine alone with him if he were truly mad? No! And you have the proof of that at the office, Counselor Agazzi, where he fulfils his duties better than all the others.

AGAZZI: That's all well and good, Signora, but you need to be a little clearer. Are we to believe that your son-in-law came here with a story completely of his own invention?

SIGNORA FROLA: Yes, oh, yes, I'll explain it all, I will, Counselor. But you must also try to understand him.

AGAZZI: But, come, now, madam! You're trying to tell us that your daughter isn't dead?

SIGNORA FROLA: *(Horrified.)* Oh, no! God forbid!

AGAZZI: *(Shouting irritatedly.)* Then it *must* be your son-in-law that's mad!

SIGNORA FROLA: *(Beseechingly.)* No, no . . . listen . . . please . . .

SIRELLI: *(Triumphantly.)* But of course! It can't be anyone else!

SIGNORA FROLA: No! Listen to me! Listen to me! He's not . . . he's not mad! Let me speak!—You've all seen him. He's a strong, powerful man; with a violent temper . . .When he married, he was seized by a veritable frenzy of love. My daughter was . . . delicate . . . and there was the possibility that he could . . . well . . . almost destroy her. On the advice of doctors and all the relatives, his own included (who now, poor souls, are all dead in the earthquake), his wife had to be taken from him without his knowing and put in a sanatorium. So then he, who naturally was already in a state because of his . . . excessive passion, and then finding her gone . . . Well, what can I say, ladies and gentlemen . . . he fell into a state of furious despair and began to believe that his wife was really dead. He refused to listen to any of us. He made up his mind to dress in black, and began to do all sorts of crazy things. There was no way of freeing his mind of this idea. Then, about a year later, my daughter had recovered and was back to being her old self and we brought her back to him. But he said no, this was not his wife. Ah! I can't even tell you the agony it cost! He'd go straight up to her and seem on the verge of recognizing her . . . and then it would be gone. The only way, with the help of friends, we could get him to take her back, was to arrange a kind of second wedding ceremony

SIGNORA SIRELLI: Ah, so that's why he says she's . . .

SIGNORA FROLA: Yes, but not even he believes it anymore—and hasn't for some time. But he still needs for others to believe it. It makes him feel more secure, you see, because he probably still has moments when he fears his wife will be taken away from him again. *(Softly, smiling confidentially.)* That's why he keeps her locked up—all to himself. But he adores her! I know he does! And my daughter is happy. *(Rises.)* I'd better go. He mustn't rush back to see me and find me out. Especially not in his agitated state. *(Sighing sweetly and waving her clasped hands from side to side.)* What can we do but be patient? My poor daughter has to pretend she's someone else. And I . . . my-o-my . . . I . . . to be crazy, dear ladies! But what can I do? As long as it gives him some peace.—No, no, please don't get up. I know the way out. My respects, dear friends, my respects. *(Bowing and saying good-bye, she hurries out the main door.)* *(The others remain standing, looking at each other in stunned amazement. Silence. LAUDISI moves into their midst.)*

LAUDISI: Look at you all! Staring at each other! Where's the truth now? *(Laughing loudly.)* Ha-ha-ha-ha!

END OF ACT I

ACT TWO

The study of Counselor Agazzi's house. Antique furniture; old pictures on the walls; entrance at the rear covered with portière; another entrance, left, also with portière, leading into the drawing room. A large fireplace is at the right, with a big mirror resting on the mantle; a telephone on the desk. A small sofa, armchairs and other chairs, etc. AGAZZI is standing by the desk, a telephone receiver to his ear. LAUDISI and SIRELLI, seated, look expectantly at him.

AGAZZI: Hello!—Yes. Is this Centuri?—Well?—Good!—Fine! *(Long pause, listening.)* I beg your . . . But how can that be possible? *(Another long pause.)* Yes, I understand; but surely with a little more . . . *(Another long pause.)* It seems very odd that you can't . . . *(Pause.)* Yes, I understand . . . yes. *(Pause.)* Yes . . . well, just see what you can do. *(Replaces the receiver and comes forward.)*

SIRELLI: *(Anxiously.)* And . . . ?

AGAZZI: Nothing.

SIRELLI: Nothing . . . ?

AGAZZI: Everything—either lost or destroyed. Town hall, archives, city records.

SIRELLI: Survivors, then. Couldn't they help?

AGAZZI: No record of any. None. And if there were, it would be no easy task to trace them.

SIRELLI: You're saying, then, that our only choice is to believe one or the other of the stories . . . without proof?

AGAZZI: It looks that way.

LAUDISI: *(Rising.)* Take my advice, and believe them both.

AGAZZI: And how do we do that if . . .

SIRELLI: . . . if one says white and the other says black?

LAUDISI: Very simple. Don't believe either of them.

SIRELLI: You must be joking! We lack proof, we lack dates, we lack facts! And yet the truth must be on one side or the other!

LAUDISI: Documented facts! Really! What would you do if you had them?

AGAZZI: Oh, come now! The daughter's death certificate, to start with. Assuming, of course, that Signora Frola is mad. Unfortunately it can't be found, nor can anything else. But it existed once, and it could turn up tomorrow. And if it does—once we have the death certificate—it would be clear that the son-in-law is right.

SIRELLI: And what if tomorrow someone handed you that document, would you really deny it as evidence?

LAUDISI: I? I deny nothing! I do my best not to! It's you who need records and documents to affirm or deny! I have no use for them! Reality, for me, is not to be found in pieces of paper, but in the minds of *those two!* *Those two* into whose minds I have no possible entry, except for the little they choose to tell me!

SIRELLI: Exactly! And doesn't each of them tell you that the other is crazy? One of the two is mad, either he or she! The question is which?

AGAZZI: That's the question, all right!

LAUDISI: First of all, it isn't true that they're both saying the other is mad. Signor Ponza, of course, says it about his mother-in-law, but Signora Frola denies it not only of herself but of him as well. At most, she claims that he was once slightly out of his mind from being too much in love. But now he's healthy and perfectly sane.

SIRELLI: Ah! Then you agree with me! You tend to side with the mother-in-law.

AGAZZI: If you go with what she says, the entire situation can be easily explained.

LAUDISI: Yes, but it can as easily be explained if you side with the son-in-law.

SIRELLI: Aha! So! Then neither one is mad! But one of them has to be, for God's sake!

LAUDISI: And which one would that be? Can't tell, can you? Neither can anyone else. And it's not because the documents you're so intent on finding have been destroyed or lost in some disaster—fire, earthquake, whatever. No. But because those two have deleted the documents from inside themselves, from their own souls. Don't you understand? She's now created for him, or he for her, a world of fantasy that has the same consistency as reality itself, and in which they live together in perfect peace and harmony. And no document whatever can destroy this reality of theirs, because they live and breathe this world. They see, they feel, they touch it! If such a document existed, what purpose would it serve, except to satisfy this foolish curiosity of yours? But it doesn't exist, and you find yourself damned to the marvelous torment of being faced on the one hand with a fantasy world and on the other with a world of reality—without being able to distinguish one from the other!

AGAZZI: You're philosophizing, old man, philosophizing! We'll soon see just how impossible it is!

SIRELLI: We listened first to one, then to the other. But what if we put them together, face-to-face, in the same room? Do you think it will still be impossible to tell fantasy from reality?

LAUDISI: All I ask is your permission to go on laughing.

AGAZZI: All right! Fine! We'll see who has the last laugh. But let's not waste more time on it. *(Goes to the door at left and calls out.)* Amalia! Signora Sirelli! You may come in now!

(Enter AMALIA, SIGNORA SIRELLI, and DINA.)

SIGNORA SIRELLI: *(To LAUDISI, with a playfully wagging finger.)* You again, Laudisi? You again?

SIRELLI: He's incorrigible!

SIGNORA SIRELLI: How ever do you avoid getting caught up in this like the rest of us? Here we are, in a frenzy to solve this mystery that's about to drive us insane! I didn't sleep a wink last night!

AGAZZI: Do yourself a favor, Signora—ignore him.

LAUDISI: By all means listen to my brother-in-law. He'll make sure you sleep tonight.

AGAZZI: All right, then. Let's get things organized here. I suggest you ladies go over to Signora Frola's . . .

AMALIA: Will she receive us?

AGAZZI: I should certainly think so!

DINA: It's our duty to return her call.

AMALIA: But he won't allow her to make or receive calls . . .

AGAZZI: Earlier, yes! When no one knew a thing. But now that she's spoken up by force of circumstance and explained the reasons for her actions . . .

SIRELLI: *(Continuing.)* . . . she'd probably be delighted to talk to us about her daughter.

DINA: And she's such a friendly old lady, too! There's no doubt in my mind whatever. He's the one who's crazy.

AGAZZI: Let's not jump to conclusions. All right, now, listen to me. *(Looks at his watch.)* Don't stay too long. A quarter of an hour at most.

SIRELLI: *(To his wife.)* Yes—and be careful about that!

SIGNORA SIRELLI: *(Growing angry.)* Why are you telling me this?

SIRELLI: You know how you are once you get to talking . . .

DINA: *(Trying to avert a quarrel between the two.)* A quarter of an hour it is, then! I'll see to it.

AGAZZI: I'm going to my office now and will be back at eleven—about twenty minutes.

SIRELLI: *(Anxiously.)* And what about me?

AGAZZI: *(Eagerly.)* One minute. *(To the ladies.)* Just before I return you'll find some excuse to bring Signora Frola back here.

AMALIA: Excuse? What excuse?

AGAZZI: Whatever! You'll think of something. Women aren't usually caught short in that area. Besides, you have Dina and Signora Sirelli to help you. You'll take her into the drawing room, of course. *(He goes to the door at the left and opens it, pulling back the portière.)* Be sure you leave the door wide open—like that—so we can hear your voices from in here. I'm leaving these papers that I should take with me to the office here on the desk. Documents drawn up specially for Ponza's attention. I'll pretend I've forgotten them as an excuse for bringing him back here. Then . . .

SIRELLI: *(Eagerly.)* Excuse me, but when do I come in?

AGAZZI: A few minutes after eleven. The ladies are in the drawing room, I'm here with Signor Ponza, and you come to pick up your wife. You'll be brought to me, and I'll invite the ladies to join us.

LAUDISI: *(Quickly.)* And the truth will be laid bare!

DINA: But surely, Uncle, when the two of them are here face-to-face . . .

AGAZZI: Oh, don't listen to him, for heaven's sake! Let's get on with this! We've no time to lose!

SIGNORA SIRELLI: Yes, come on, let's go! *(To LAUDISI.)* As for you, I'm not even going to say good-bye.

LAUDISI: Then I'll just have to say good-bye to myself *for* you! *(Shakes hands with himself.)* Good luck!

(AMALIA, DINA, and SIGNORA SIRELLI go off.)

AGAZZI: *(To SIRELLI.)* I suppose we should be on our way, too, mm? Right!

SIRELLI: Right! Good-bye, Lamberto!

LAUDISI: Good-bye, good-bye!

(AGAZZI and SIRELLI go off. Alone, LAUDISI saunters around the study, smiling derisively to himself and shaking his head. Eventually he stops in front of the large mirror resting on the mantle, looks at his image in it, and begins speaking to it.)

LAUDISI: Ah, so there you are! *(Waves two fingers in greeting, winks cunningly, and laughs sarcastically.)* So, tell me, old boy! Which of the two of us is crazy? *(Raises a hand and points the index finger at his image which points back at him. Another sarcastic laugh and he continues.)* Yes, well, I know. I say: "It's you!" and you point right back at me with *your* finger. Well, why not just agree that each of us knows the other pretty well by this time, eh? The problem is that others don't see you quite the way I do. So, then, what's to become of you, old friend? Standing here in front of you I see myself and touch myself. But you? What do you become? For the others? A ghost, old boy, a ghost! But do you see all these crazy people? These people who pay no attention to their own ghost, the one they carry around inside them day and night? And what do they do? They chase around like fools after other people's ghosts, fully convinced that it's something quite different from theirs!

(The BUTLER, having entered, hears the final words of LAUDISI's speech to the mirror, then addresses him.)

BUTLER: Signor Lamberto.

LAUDISI: Yes?

BUTLER: There are two ladies at the door. Signora Cini and another.

LAUDISI: Do they want to see me?

BUTLER: They asked for the mistress. I told them she was visiting Signora Frola next door, and then . . .

LAUDISI: Then?

BUTLER: They looked at each other, fidgeted with their glove, saying, "Oh, is she, is she?" Finally they asked very excitedly if there was anyone at home at all.

LAUDISI: And you said there was no one?

BUTLER: I said that only you were here.

LAUDISI: Me? No. Not at all. And *if* at all, it's the me they think they know, not the real me.

BUTLER: *(More annoyed than ever.)* What was that, Signore?

LAUDISI: Excuse me, but can't you tell them apart?

BUTLER: *(As before; with a miserable attempt at a slack-jawed smile.)* I don't understand, Signore.

LAUDISI: Who are you talking to?

BUTLER: *(Dumbfounded.)* I'm sorry, Signore, I don't . . . who am I talking to? To you . . .

LAUDISI: Yes, but are you certain I'm the same person those ladies want to see?

BUTLER: Well, I don't . . . I don't know . . . they said the mistress' brother.

LAUDISI: Ah, well, my dear man! In that case it's me, all right! It's me they want to see. Show them in, show them in . . .

(The BUTLER goes out while turning his head several times to look back at LAUDISI as if to say he no longer believes his eyes. SIGNORA CINI and SIGNORA NENNI enter a moment later.)

SIGNORA CINI: May I come in?

LAUDISI: By all means, Signora, please, come in.

SIGNORA CINI: I take it that Signora Agazzi is not at home. I've brought my friend Signora Nenni. *(She introduces her: an even more awkward and affected old lady than SIGNORA CINI herself, and like her full of greedy curiosity, but at the same time guarded and reticent.)* She was so longing to meet Signora—

LAUDISI: *(Quickly.)* Frola?

SIGNORA CINI: No, no! Your sister!

LAUDISI: Oh, she'll be here. Yes, absolutely. In just a while. Signora Frola, too. Please. Make yourselves comfortable. *(He invites them to sit on the small sofa, then gracefully manages to squeeze himself in to sit between them.)* I hope you don't mind. The sofa sits three quite comfortably, I think. Signora Sirelli also went over with them.

SIGNORA CINI: Yes, yes, the butler mentioned it.

LAUDISI: It's all been orchestrated, you know. Ah, what a scene it will be! Really marvelous! Any minute now, right at eleven. In this very room.

SIGNORA CINI: *(Bewildered.)* Orchestrated? I don't . . . What?

LAUDISI: *(Mysteriously, first by raising both hands and bringing together the tips of his index fingers, then with his voice.)* The confrontation! *(With an admiring gesture.)* What a grand idea!

SIGNORA CINI: What . . . what confrontation?

LAUDISI: Them! The two of them! He'll first be brought into this room.

SIGNORA CINI: Signor Ponza?

LAUDISI: Yes. And she'll be over there in that room. *(Points at the drawing-room.)*

SIGNORA CINI: Signora Frola?

LAUDISI: Yes, Signora. *(Once again, first with an expressive gesture of the hand, and then with his voice.)* Think of it! Getting the pair of them in here, face-to-face! While we sit around watching and listening! What a first-class idea!

SIGNORA CINI: Which will lead to . . . ?

LAUDISI: To the truth! But we know that already, of course. All that's left for us now is the unmasking!

SIGNORA CINI: *(Surprised and very anxiously.)* Ah! Then they know? Who is it? Which of the two? Who?

LAUDISI: Well, let's see, now. Why don't you guess? Which of them do you think it is?

SIGNORA CINI: *(Chuckling but hesitant.)* Well . . . really . . . I . . .

LAUDISI: He or she? Go on, guess! Don't be afraid!

SIGNORA CINI: I . . . I say . . . he is!

LAUDISI: *(Looks at her before replying.)* It's him, all right!

SIGNORA CINI: *(Chuckling elatedly.)* Yes? It is? It is! Of course! Of course! Who else could it be!

SIGNORA NENNI: *(Chuckling elatedly.)* It's him! All of us women said so!

SIGNORA CINI: But how, how did you find this out? Documents, I suppose? Proof?

SIGNORA NENNI: Police headquarters, surely. It's just what we were saying. With the prefecture behind it something was certain to be found.

LAUDISI: *(Motions them to come closer; then speaks softly and mysteriously, weighing every syllable.)* The certificate for the second marriage.

SIGNORA CINI: *(As though she had received a blow to the face.)* The *second?*

SIGNORA NENNI: *(Very upset.)* The . . . the what? The second marriage?

SIGNORA CINI: *(Recovering, crossly.)* But then . . . then he was right after all!

LAUDISI: Documents, dear ladies, documents! The certificate for the second marriage speaks clearly enough, I dare say.

SIGNORA NENNI: *(On the verge of tears.)* Then she's the one who's mad?

LAUDISI: It would certainly seem so.

SIGNORA CINI: But how? First you say it's him, then her!

LAUDISI: Yes. But you see, my dear madam, the second marriage certificate just might be a fake. After all, Signora Frola has assured us it is. A certificate forged with the help of friends to support him in his delusion that his present wife is not her daughter, but another woman entirely.

SIGNORA CINI: Ah, then a public document can be worthless?

LAUDISI: Well . . . yes and no. I mean, it's value is what each of you ladies wants to give it. For example, the letters that Signora Frola claims her daughter delivers to her by basket every day in the courtyard. We admit, don't we, that these letters exist?

SIGNORA CINI: Yes, and . . . ?

LAUDISI: Well, then—documents, Signora! These little letters are documents, too. It all depends on the value you want to give them. Signor Ponza comes forward claiming they're forgeries to support Signora Frola's delusion—

SIGNORA CINI: Oh my, mercy, then . . . then there's nothing we can be certain of.

LAUDISI: Nothing? Well . . . perhaps we shouldn't exaggerate! The days of the week, for example. How many are there?

SIGNORA CINI: Mm, um, seven.

LAUDISI: Monday, Tuesday, Wednesday . . .

SIGNORA CINI: *(Invited to continue.)* Thursday, Friday, Saturday . . .

LAUDISI: And Sunday! *(Turning to SIGNORA NENNI.)* And the months of the year?

SIGNORA NENNI: Twelve!

LAUDISI: January, February, March . . .

SIGNORA CINI: That will be quite enough! You're only trying to make fun of us!

DINA: *(Enters, running, through the doorway at the rear.)* Uncle, please, we . . . *(She stops short on seeing SIGNORA CINI.)* Oh! Signora Cini! You're here!

SIGNORA CINI: Yes, I came with Signora Nenni . . .

LAUDISI: . . . who is anxious to meet Signora Frola.

SIGNORA NENNI: No, I'm sorry, that's not . . .

SIGNORA CINI: He just can't help poking fun at us! Ah, my dear, dear girl, he just never lets up! It's like being on a train entering a station: ba-boom, ba-boom, switching endlessly from track to track. We're utterly dazed.

DINA: Yes, he's been naughty with us, too, lately. Just be patient. I suppose I won't be needing anything else, Uncle. I'll go tell Mama who's here, and that will be that.—But you should hear her, Uncle. What a sweet old lady she is. The way she talks. So kind. And that little apartment of hers—clean and tidy as a whistle, everything in place, and the little white embroidered doilies on the furniture. She even showed us her daughter's letters.

SIGNORA CINI: Yes . . . well . . . but if, as Signor Laudisi was saying . . .

DINA: But what can he know? He hasn't read them!

SIGNORA CINI: But couldn't they be fakes?

DINA: Fakes? You must be joking! Don't pay him any mind! How could a mother be fooled by her own daughter's expressions? Why, the latest letter, written only yesterday—*(She is interrupted by the sound of voices from the drawing room.)* Ah, but here they are—I think they've arrived! *(She goes to the drawing room door to look.)*

SIGNORA CINI: *(Hurries after her.)* Is she there, too? Signora Frola?

DINA: Yes. Come along now, come with me. We all have to be in the drawing room. Is it eleven yet, Uncle?

AMALIA: *(Rushing in from the drawing room in an agitated state.)* I think we know all we need to know! No need for further proof!

DINA: I agree. Yes. To continue would be ridiculous.

AMALIA: *(Sorry and anxious, hastily greets SIGNORA CINI.)* How do you do, Signora.

SIGNORA CINI: *(Introducing SIGNORA NENNI.)* Signora Nenni, who came with me to . . .

AMALIA: *(Also hastily greeting SIGNORA NENNI.)* Delighted, Signora! *(Then.)* No doubt about it! He's the one!

SIGNORA CINI: He's the one? It's true, then? He's the one?

DINA: If only we could stop Papa playing this awful trick on that poor old lady!

AMALIA: I know! Now that we've brought her here I feel as if I'm betraying her!

LAUDISI: That's exactly what it is! An unworthy and outrageous trick! You're right! Especially since it's so obvious that she *has* to be the one who's mad! I'm certain of it!

AMALIA: She? But how? What are you saying?

LAUDISI: She, she, she!

AMALIA: Oh, will you stop!

DINA: And we're fully convinced of the opposite!

SIGNORA CINI and SIGNORA NENNI: *(Giggling.)* You are, aren't you! Yes, you are!

LAUDISI: I'm certain she's the one because you're so certain she isn't!

DINA: Oh, let's go into the other room. He's just doing this on purpose!

AMALIA: Yes, let's. Let's go. *(Standing at the door on the left.)* This way, ladies. *(SIGNORA CINI, SIGNORA NENNI, and AMALIA go out. DINA is about to follow when LAUDISI calls out to her.)*

LAUDISI: Dina!

DINA: I won't listen to you! No, no, no!

LAUDISI: If you have all the proof you want, why not shut the door?

DINA: And Papa? What about him? He's the one who left it open. He'll be here any moment with that man. What if he found it shut? You know how Papa is!

LAUDISI: You and your mother—but you especially—can persuade him that there was no reason to keep it open. Aren't you convinced?

DINA: Absolutely!

LAUDISI: *(With a challenging smile.)* Then shut it!

DINA: You want to plunge me into a spectacle of indecision, don't you? But you won't. And I won't shut it. But only because of Papa.

LAUDISI: *(As above.)* Shall *I* shut it, then?

DINA: On your own responsibility!

LAUDISI: But I don't share your certainty that he's the one who's mad.

DINA: If you'd only come into the drawing room with me and hear the old lady out, as we have, you'd soon realize that you have no doubts either. Will you?

LAUDISI: Yes, of course. And I'll also shut the door. On my own responsibility.

DINA: There, you see? And even before you've heard a word.

LAUDISI: No, my dear. But because by this time your father will have arrived at the same conclusion as you—that this test is no longer needed.

DINA: You're certain of that?

LAUDISI: Of course! At this very moment he's talking to Signor Ponza, and has been convinced that it's Signora Frola that's mad. So . . . *(Walking resolutely to the door.)* I shut the door.

DINA: *(Stopping him in his tracks.)* No. *(Then.)* I'm sorry. If you really think so . . . we'll leave it open . . .

LAUDISI: *(With his usual laughter.)* Ha-ha-ha!

DINA: Only for Papa's sake!

LAUDISI: And Papa will say it's for your sake!—We'll leave it open.
(The sound of a piano is heard coming from the other room: an old aria full of melancholy grace and sadness from Paisiello's "Nina, pazza per amore.")

DINA: Ah, there she is . . . Listen. She's playing. Really playing!

LAUDISI: The old lady?

DINA: Yes. She was saying that her daughter always used to play that same old tune. How sweetly she plays! Come, let's go in.
(They leave through the door at the left. The stage is empty for a while as the piano continues in the drawing room. SIGNOR PONZA, entering with COUNSELOR AGAZZI through the door at the rear, hears the music and becomes deeply disturbed; his emotion grows increasingly as the scene progresses.)

AGAZZI: *(At the doorway.)* Do go in, please. *(Seeing him in, he goes to the desk for the papers he pretends to have forgotten.)* They must be here somewhere. Do have a seat, Signor Ponza. *(SIGNOR PONZA remains standing, looking agitatedly toward the room from which the music is coming.)* Yes, yes, here they are. I knew they would be. *(Picking up the file, he goes toward SIGNOR PONZA, leafing through the pages.)* As I was saying, it's quite a tangled affair that's been dragging on for years. *(Also irritated by the music, he turns in the direction of the drawing room.)* That music! What a time to be playing! *(He turns back to PONZA with a deprecating gesture that seems to say "Stupid women!")* Who can that be? *(Looking through the door into the drawing room he sees SIGNORA FROLA at the piano and registers amazement.)* Good lord!

PONZA: *(Approaching AGAZZI, agitated.)* In the name of God, is *she* here? Is that her playing?

AGAZZI: Yes, your mother-in-law. She plays well.

PONZA: What is all this? You've brought her back here again? And you're making her play the piano?

AGAZZI: I see no harm in that.

PONZA: Sweet Jesus, but not that music! It's what her daughter used to play!

AGAZZI: You find it painful to listen to, then?

PONZA: Painful, yes! But not for me! For her! Incalculable pain! I've explained it to you, Counselor, as I have to the ladies, the situation that poor, unfortunate woman finds herself in—

AGAZZI: *(Trying to calm him as he grows increasingly more agitated.)* Yes . . . you're quite right . . . but you see—

PONZA: *(Continuing.)* —she must be left in peace! Must have no visitors but me, only me. And she must make no visits! I alone understand how she must be treated! You're destroying her! Destroying her!

AGAZZI: I'm afraid I can't agree. My wife and daughter are perfectly aware that . . . *(He breaks off momentarily when the music in the next room stops and a burst of applause is heard.)* There! You see? Listen to that!
(The following exchange is clearly heard from the drawing room.)

DINA: How well you still play, Signora!

SIGNORA FROLA: I? Oh, no! Ah, but my Lina! You should hear how beautifully my Lina plays!

PONZA: *(Trembling, wringing his hands.)* Her Lina! Did you hear? *Her* Lina, she said!

AGAZZI: Yes, of course . . . her daughter.

PONZA: But she said *plays! Plays!*
(SIGNORA FROLA is again heard clearly from the drawing room.)

SIGNORA FROLA: Well, no, she doesn't play anymore, you see, not since it happened. And probably that's what gives her the greatest pain, poor thing!

AGAZZI: Seems all quite natural to me. She believes her daughter's still alive . . .

PONZA: But they shouldn't allow her to say such things! She shouldn't . . . she mustn't say such things! You heard what she said: "not since it happened." She said it! She meant *that* piano! Not that you could know about it! The piano that belonged to my poor dead wife!
(SIRELLI enters to hear the last of PONZA's words and to note his state of

extreme exasperation. He stands, struck dumb, at the door. AGAZZI, also bewildered, motions him forward.)

AGAZZI: *(To SIRELLI.)* Please ask the ladies to come in.

(SIRELLI, keeping his distance from PONZA, goes to the door at the left and calls to the ladies.)

SIRELLI: Ladies, if you please!

PONZA: Ladies? In here? No, no! I'd rather . . .

(At a sign from the amazed SIRELLI, the ladies enter somewhat frightened. When SIGNORA FROLA catches sight of her son-in-law in his state of extreme excitement, quivering with near-animal fury, she becomes frightened. In the following scene he will attack her with extraordinary violence, at which she will exchange knowing glances with the other ladies. The tempo of the scene is rapid and highly excitable.)

PONZA: You, here? Again? What are you doing here?

SIGNORA FROLA: I . . . I came . . . but don't be angry . . .

PONZA: You came to tell some more of your . . . What have you said? What have you told these ladies?

SIGNORA FROLA: Nothing, I swear! Nothing!

PONZA: Nothing? Nothing!? I heard you myself! This gentleman heard it, too! *(Indicating AGAZZI.)* You said "she plays"! *Who* plays? Lina plays? The same Lina, your daughter, who's been dead for four years, as you very well know?

SIGNORA FROLA: Of course! Of course she has, my dear! Don't get so excited! There, there . . .

PONZA: "She doesn't play anymore, not since it happened," you said! Of course she doesn't play anymore, how could she, when she's dead?

SIGNORA FROLA: There, you see? That's it! Isn't that what I said, ladies? That she couldn't play anymore, not since it happened? How could she? When she's dead?

PONZA: Then why are you always talking about that old piano?

SIGNORA FROLA: I don't! I don't! I never think about it!

PONZA: I destroyed it! I smashed it! As you know very well! Smashed it to pieces! When your daughter died! So the other one couldn't play it! The other who doesn't know one note from another! As you well know!

SIGNORA FROLA: That's right! Not one note from another!

PONZA: Her name! What was it? Your daughter's name? Lina? That's it, isn't it? And what's my second wife's name? I want you to tell them, here, now, my second wife's name! Tell everyone! You know it as well as you know your own! What's her name?

SIGNORA FROLA: Julia! Her name is Julia! Yes, it's true, exactly—Julia!

PONZA: Yes, Julia, not Lina! And you can stop your winking when you say that—when you say her name is Julia!

SIGNORA FROLA: But I didn't—I didn't! Did I wink?

PONZA: I saw you! You winked! I saw it myself! You're out to ruin me! To make them think I want to keep your daughter all to myself—as if she wasn't dead. *(Bursting into terrible sobs.)* As if she wasn't dead!

SIGNORA FROLA: *(Rushing toward him with infinite tenderness and humility.)* No, no, no, never—I never did, my dear, dear boy, I never said she was alive, never! Calm down, now . . . there, there, my dear. I never said so, did I, ladies? Did I? It's true!

AMALIA, SIGNORA SIRELLI, and DINA: Well, of course not! No! She said no such thing! Certainly not! She always said her daughter was dead!

SIGNORA FROLA: It's true, then! Yes? I always said she was dead! Of course I did! What else? And how good you are to me! *(To the ladies.)* It's true, isn't it? It's true? *(To PONZA.)* Ruin you? Why would I want to? Why would I do such a thing?

PONZA: *(Bristling with a terrible rage.)* In the meanwhile you go ransacking people's houses for pianos to play your daughter's tunes on, saying she plays like that, only better!

SIGNORA FROLA: No, that's not . . . I only did it . . . I only did it to prove . . .

PONZA: No, but you can't! You mustn't! How can you play the same music your dead daughter used to play?

SIGNORA FROLA: No, no, you're right, you're right, you poor . . . you poor, dear thing! *(Overcome by tenderness, she begins to cry.)* I'll never do it again . . . never . . .

PONZA: *(Standing very close, attacks her viciously.)* Go! Get out of here! Go! Go!

SIGNORA FROLA: Yes . . . yes . . .I'll go, I'm going . . . Oh, God!

(As she moves, tearfully, to leave, she makes imploring gestures to everyone to be kind to her son-in-law. When she is gone, all present are left staring at PONZA with a mixture of pity and fear, at which he regains his conventional composure of total calm.)

PONZA: *(Very simply.)* You must excuse this sad spectacle, ladies and gentlemen. I had no choice. The harm you did had to be undone. Harm which, of course, you inflicted without knowing or wanting to, and which you did out of the purest sympathy for this unfortunate woman.

AGAZZI: *(Amazed along with all the others.)* I don't understand. You were pretending?

PONZA: I had no choice, my friends. This is the only way to keep her illusion in tact. Don't you see that? Yelling the truth into her face as if it were my own mad fantasy? Please forgive me, and allow me to leave now. I have to see to her at once. *(PONZA leaves by the main door, leaving the others staring at each other in silent bewilderment.)*

LAUDISI: *(Making his way into their midst.)* There we have it, then, ladies and gentlemen! The truth laid bare! *(Bursting into laughter.)* Ha-ha-ha-ha!

END OF ACT II

ACT THREE

The study of Counselor Agazzi's house as in the second act. LAUDISI is stretched out in an easy chair, reading. From the door at the left leading into the drawing room is heard the sound of many voices. The BUTLER appears at the upstage door and leads in COMMISSIONER CENTURI.

BUTLER: Wait here, please. I'll tell the Counselor of your arrival.

LAUDISI: *(Turning catches sight of CENTURI.)* Ah, it's you, Commissioner! *(Rising quickly he calls to the BUTLER who is about to enter the drawing room.)* Pst! Wait! *(To CENTURI.)* Any news?

CENTURI: *(Tall, stiff, frowning, about forty years old.)* Yes, some.

LAUDISI: Ah, good! *(To the BUTLER.)* Never mind. I'll go in there later and fetch my brother-in-law. *(Indicates the door to the drawing room with a movement of his head.)* You've just brought about a miracle! Saved a whole town! Listen to them! Shouting! Solid facts, I assume?

CENTURI: Well, we've at least finally tracked someone down.

LAUDISI: From Signor Ponza's village? Some neighbor who knows the facts?

CENTURI: Yes, sir. A few facts—not many—but quite definite.

LAUDISI: Good! Very good! For example?

CENTURI: Yes. Well. Here are the communications I've received. *(He takes from an inside jacket pocket an unsealed yellow envelope containing a single sheet of paper and hands it to LAUDISI.)*

LAUDISI: Let's see here! Let's see! *(He removes the sheet of paper and proceeds to read it carefully, interpolating from time to time little exclamations such as "ah" and "eh" in various tones of voice, expressing in order satisfaction, then doubt, then something resembling pity, and finally total disillusionment.)* But there's nothing here! Not a definite fact in this entire report, Commissioner!

CENTURI: It's all we've been able to find out.

LAUDISI: But all the doubts are still there! *(Looks at him for a moment and comes to a sudden decision.)* Commissioner! How would you like to do something really good? Do your fellow-citizens an outstanding service? One for which the good Lord will surely reward you?

CENTURI: *(Looking at him perplexed.)* What service is that? I don't know.

LAUDISI: Then let me tell you. Sit here. *(Indicates the desk.)* Now tear that sheet of paper in two. It's useless. And throw away the half with your report that proves nothing. On the other half, however, you will write something that is clear, precise, and meaningful.

CENTURI: *(Stunned.)* I don't . . . But how? What information?

LAUDISI: Any information at all. Suit yourself! Anything! But write it in the name of those two fellow countrymen that you've tracked down. Do it for the good of everyone! To return peace and quiet to the old town! It's truth they want—every one of them—and which truth is of absolutely no importance, as long as it's something specific, categorical. You're the one who can do it! Give it to them!

CENTURI: *(Forcefully; growing heated; almost offended.)* But how can I give them what I don't have? You want me to commit forgery? I'm stunned you could propose such a thing! And that's putting it rather weakly! So you will kindly announce to Signor Agazzi at once that I am here.

LAUDISI: *(Spreads his arms in defeat.)* Yes, of course! At once! *(Crosses to the door at the left and opens it. The shouting from the drawing room suddenly becomes louder. But the moment that LAUDISI steps into the room there is a sudden silence, and from the drawing room his voice is heard making the following announcement.)* Ladies and gentlemen, Commissioner Centuri is here with specific information from people who are informed of the facts!

(Applause and cheering greet the news. COMMISSIONER CENTURI is visibly distressed, knowing that the information he has will in no way satisfy their expectations. Enter AGAZZI, SIRELLI, LAUDISI, AMALIA, DINA, SIGNORA SIRELLI, SIGNORA CINI, SIGNORA NENNI, and many other ladies and gentlemen. All rush through the door to the drawing room, led on by AGAZZI. They are excited, exultant, clap their hands and shout: "Bravo! Well done, Centuri!")

AGAZZI: *(Both hands extended.)* Good old Centuri, I knew you could do it! Knew you couldn't help but come out on top!

ALL: Bravo! Bravo, Centuri! Let's hear it! Let's hear! Let's see the proof! Which one is it? Who?

CENTURI: *(Stunned, bewildered, dismayed.)* Well, no . . . you see . . . I . . . I mean, Counselor . . .

AGAZZI: Ladies and gentlemen, please! Give him a chance! Quiet, please!

CENTURI: It's true, I've done my best, of course; but when Signor Laudisi tells you that . . .

AGAZZI: . . . that you bring us definite information!

SIRELLI: Precise facts!

LAUDISI: *(Loud, resolute, anticipating.)* Perhaps not many facts, it's true, but precise facts. People he has tracked down! From Signor Ponza's village! People who know what happened!

ALL: Finally! Ah, at last! At last!

CENTURI: *(Shrugging his shoulders and handing the sheet to AGAZZI.)* There—for you—you have it now, Counselor.

AGAZZI: *(Unfolds the sheet of paper surrounded by the crowd that has rushed to him.)* Let's see here! Let's see!

CENTURI: *(Resentful, coming up to LAUDISI.)* But you, Signor Laudisi . . .

LAUDISI: *(Quickly, in a loud voice.)* Let him read, for God's sake, let him read!

AGAZZI: Ladies and gentlemen, be patient, please! Give me some room! There! I'll read it as quickly as possible.

(A moment of silence, which is then broken by the loud, clear voice of LAUDISI.)

LAUDISI: I know what it says! I've read it!

ALL: *(Leave AGAZZI and crowd around LAUDISI.)* You have? Well, then! What does it say? Tell us what it says!

LAUDISI: *(Choosing his words carefully.)* On the testimony of a fellow townsman of Signor Ponza, there is incontestable proof that Signora Frola has been in a sanatorium!

ALL: *(With regret and disappointment.)* Oh!

SIGNORA SIRELLI: Signora Frola?

DINA: She's the one, then?

AGAZZI: *(Now finished reading the document, waving the paper in the air and shouting.)* No, no! Not so! It says nothing like that here!

ALL: *(Leave LAUDISI and crowd back around AGAZZI.)* What's that? What does it say? What is it?

LAUDISI: *(Loudly to AGAZZI.)* But it does! It says "the Signora"! It specifically says "the Signora"!

AGAZZI: *(Even more loudly.)* It's nothing of the sort! The gentleman in question says: "It seems to him!" He makes no pretense to being certain. He doesn't even know if it was the daughter or the mother who was sent to the sanatorium.

ALL: *(With satisfaction.)* Ah!

LAUDISI: *(Insistently.)* But it has to be the mother! There can be no doubt!

SIRELLI: No! The daughter, gentlemen! It has to be the daughter!

SIGNORA SIRELLI: Which is exactly what the Signora herself told us!

AMALIA: Well, there you are, then! Excellent! It was when they took her away from her husband without telling him . . .

DINA: . . . and placed her in a sanatorium!

AGAZZI: But the witness isn't even from the right town! He admits he went

there often enough . . . but he doesn't really remember all that well . . .
he seems to recall some discussion or other . . .

SIRELLI: In which case it's all just hearsay!

LAUDISI: Do excuse me, but if you are all so convinced that Signora Frola
is right, why are you still looking for proof? End it once and for all, for
God's sake! He's the one who's crazy, and that's that!

SIRELLI: That's all well and good, my dear man, except that the Prefect sees
it as quite the opposite and has openly sided with Signor Ponza! He sup-
ports him totally!

CENTURI: That's true, gentlemen! The Prefect does believe Signor Ponza's
story. He told me so himself.

AGAZZI: And yet the Prefect hasn't yet spoken to the woman next door to us!

SIGNORA SIRELLI: No, he certainly hasn't. Only with him! Only with
Ponza!

SIRELLI: The fact is, there are others in this room who think exactly as the
Prefect.

A GENTLEMAN: And I'm one of them. I know of a case just like this.
Where a mother went crazy over the death of her daughter, and now
believes that her son-in-law won't let her see her. The same thing exactly.

SECOND GENTLEMAN: No, sorry, not quite the same. The son-in-law
you're talking about never remarried and is living alone. Signor Ponza,
on the other hand, has a woman living with him at home . . .

LAUDISI: (Suddenly struck by a new thought.) Good God, did you hear that?
There it is, ladies and gentlemen! The clue we've been looking for—that
solves our mystery! Good God! You've found it! The answer! (Slapping
the SECOND GENTLEMAN on the back.) I congratulate you, sir!
Everybody—did you hear?

ALL: (Perplexed, not understanding.) What does he mean? What?

SECOND GENTLEMAN: (Dazed.) What did I say? I don't . . .

LAUDISI: What did you say! Oh, come, now! You've solved it! The problem!
Just take it slow, ladies and gentlemen, just take it slow! (To AGAZZI.)
Will the Prefect be arriving here by any chance?

AGAZZI: Yes, we're expecting him . . . But why do you ask? Explain yourself!

LAUDISI: It makes no sense whatever his coming here to speak with Signora
Frola. At present he believes the son-in-law's story. Let him speak with
the mother-in-law and he'll be as confused as we are about who to
believe! No, no! Something quite different is required of the Prefect in
this case. Something that only he can do!

ALL: What? What do you mean? What?

LAUDISI: *(Radiant.)* But don't you see? Didn't you hear what this gentleman said? Signor Ponza has "a woman" living with him! The wife.

SIRELLI: Get the wife to talk, you mean? Of course! Why not!

DINA: But she's kept locked up like a prisoner, poor thing!

SIRELLI: The Prefect will simply assert his authority and order her to talk!

AMALIA: There's certainly no one else who can give us the truth!

SIGNORA SIRELLI: Not quite! No! She'll say what her husband tells her to say!

LAUDISI: If she speaks in his presence, yes. Undoubtedly!

SIRELLI: She'll have to speak with the Prefect in private.

AGAZZI: In which case the Prefect will be able to bring his authority to bear and insist she tell him, quite confidentially, what the situation in fact is! What do you think of that, Centuri?

CENTURI: Yes, certainly . . . provided, of course, it's what the Prefect wants.

AGAZZI: There's really nothing else to do. We'll need to alert him to this and spare him the inconvenience of coming here. I trust you'll see to that, Centuri?

CENTURI: Yes, Signore! My compliments, ladies and gentlemen! *(He bows on his way out.)*

SIGNORA SIRELLI: *(Clapping her hands.)* Of course! Bravo, Laudisi!

DINA: Bravo, Uncle, bravo! What a grand idea!

ALL: Bravo! Bravo! It's the only way! The only way!

AGAZZI: Of course! Why didn't we think of it before this?

SIRELLI: Yes, well! But no one's ever seen her! It's as if the poor woman never existed!

LAUDISI: *(As if struck by a new idea.)* Ah! Excuse me! Excuse me! But are you really certain she exists?

AMALIA: Lamberto! What are you saying! Good God!

SIRELLI: *(Faking laughter.)* You're now beginning to doubt her existence?

LAUDISI: Not so fast there—slow down! You said yourselves that no one's ever seen her!

DINA: Nonsense! Signora Frola sees and talks to her every day!

SIGNORA SIRELLI: A fact that the son-in-law would support as well.

LAUDISI: True! Yes! But just think for a moment! Logically there should be nothing but a ghost living in that flat.

ALL: A ghost?

AGAZZI: Oh, let's do put a lid on it! Once and for all?

LAUDISI: No, now, just let me finish! That's right, a ghost! The ghost of a second wife, if Signora Frola is correct; or the ghost of Signora Frola's daughter, if Signor Ponza is to be believed. What remains to be seen, my friends, is whether, for either of them, the ghost exists as a person in her own right. And considering the current state of our knowledge, I should say that there is good reason for doubt!

AMALIA: Oh, really! You want to drive us all as mad as you are!

SIGNORA NENNI: Oh, God, I'm all goose bumps!

SIGNORA CINI: Do you enjoy frightening us like that?

ALL: No! Of course not! He's joking! It's a joke!

SIRELLI: She's a woman of flesh and blood—no doubt about it! And we'll make her talk—hear what she has to say.

AGAZZI: *(To LAUDISI.)* And you were the one suggested she talk to the Prefect!

LAUDISI: Yes, of course, of course I did. Assuming there really *is* a woman up there—an ordinary woman, that is. But consider carefully, my friends. There can't possibly be an ordinary woman up in that flat. Impossible! At least I now have very grave doubts about it.

SIGNORA SIRELLI: Good God, he really does want to drive us all mad!

LAUDISI: Well, we'll see. We'll see.

ALL: *(Confused.)* But other people have seen her! She looks down into the courtyard! She writes letters! He's doing it on purpose! Making fools of us!

CENTURI: *(Returns during the confusion, very excitedly, and announces.)* The Prefect! The Prefect is coming!

AGAZZI: What? Here? But what did you . . .

CENTURI: He was already on his way, on the street, with Signor Ponza, when I—

SIRELLI: Aha, with Signor Ponza!

AGAZZI: Oh, God! If Ponza's with him, he'll head straight to Signora Frola next door! Please, Centuri, wait outside the door. And when he arrives ask him to drop in here for a moment first, as he promised he would.

CENTURI: Of course, Signore. I'm on my way. *(Hurries out the main door.)*

AGAZZI: Ladies and gentlemen, be so kind as to move into the drawing room for a moment.

SIGNORA SIRELLI: You will be direct with him, won't you. It's the only way! The only way!

AMALIA: *(At the door on the left.)* Right this way, ladies, if you please.

AGAZZI: Stay here, Sirelli. And you, too, Lamberto. *(Waiting till all the others have left the room.)* Leave the talking to me.

LAUDISI: Quite all right with me. I can even leave the room, if you like . . .

AGAZZI: No, no. It's better you stay.—Ah, here he is now.
(*The PREFECT enters. He is a man of sixty, tall, fat, with an air of bon-homie. CENTURI follows.*)
PREFECT: Dear Agazzi! Ah, and you, too, Sirelli! My dear Laudisi! (*Shakes hands with each of them.*)
AGAZZI: (*Inviting him to sit.*) Excuse me for asking you to come here first.
PREFECT: Not at all, I'd intended to, as I promised. At the least afterwards.
AGAZZI: (*Noticing CENTURI a few steps behind him.*) Come, Centuri. Sit here, why don't you.
PREFECT: So. Sirelli. From what I hear, you're more than a little disturbed over the gossip regarding our new secretary.
SIRELLI: Not the only one, Prefect. The whole town is up in arms.
AGAZZI: He's right, Signore, yes, everyone is disturbed.
PREFECT: Yes, and I can't quite understand why.
AGAZZI: That's because you haven't seen what we've seen. With the mother-in-law living right next to us.
SIRELLI: Begging your pardon, Signore. You haven't heard what that poor old woman has to say.
PREFECT: I was just on my way there. (*To AGAZZI.*) I know I promised to talk to her here at your place, as you asked; but then the son-in-law came and begged—actually implored me—to go to her place and end all this gossip. I'm sorry, but do you really think he'd have done this if he weren't certain the visit would provide proof for his own story?
AGAZZI: Oh, certainly! With him there, the poor old thing—
SIRELLI: (*Cutting in.*) —would say exactly what he wants her to say! And that alone proves she isn't the one who's mad!
AGAZZI: We had a demonstration of that here yesterday.
PREFECT: Well, of course, my boy. That's because he deliberately makes her believe that he's the crazy one. He warned me about that. Otherwise how could he keep the poor woman in her illusion? It's a torment for him, believe me, a real torment, the poor man!
SIRELLI: Yes! Absolutely! Unless, of course, you assume the illusion is his—an illusion fostered by *her*, of course—that her daughter is dead—so that he can feel certain that his wife won't be taken from him again! In which case, you see, Prefect, the torment would be hers, not his!
AGAZZI: And that's where the doubt comes in. And when it does, when it enters the mind—
SIRELLI: —as it has everyone's—
PREFECT: Doubt? No, I don't think so. In the first place, I don't see the

faintest shadow of a doubt in any of your minds. And as for me—though I come from the opposite direction—there's none either. What about you, Laudisi?

LAUDISI: Sorry, Signore. I've promised my brother-in-law to keep my mouth shut.

AGAZZI: *(Jumping in.)* Oh, come off it! What's got into you! *(To the PRE-FECT.)* I admit, I asked him to keep quiet, and do you know why? For the past two days he's done nothing but have fun with us, stirring things up and simply confusing the issue!

LAUDISI: Nothing of the sort, Prefect! I've done everything possible, in fact, to clarify the issue!

SIRELLI: And just how has he done *that?* I'll tell you! By insisting that the truth is beyond discovery, and then by suggesting that Signor Ponza is living not with a woman of flesh and blood, but with a ghost!

PREFECT: *(Fully amused.)* My, my! Oh, how marvelous!

AGAZZI: So there you have it! Listening to him is a total waste of time!

LAUDISI: And yet, Prefect, it was I who suggested inviting you here!

PREFECT: And do you also think I should speak with the woman next door?

LAUDISI: Bless me, no! I think you're far better sticking with Signor Ponza's story!

PREFECT: Ah, good! Then you agree that Signor Ponza is . . .

LAUDISI: *(Quickly.)* No. And I also believe the people here should continue believing Signora Frola's story—and let that be an end!

AGAZZI: Do you get the picture? Do you call that reasoning?

PREFECT: Allow me . . . *(To LAUDISI.)* According to you, then, we should also believe the old lady's story?

LAUDISI: Oh, absolutely! Every word of it! The same as his—Signor Ponza's!

PREFECT: Excuse me . . . but . . . where does that take us?

SIRELLI: After all, they *do* contradict each other!

AGAZZI: *(Irritated, determined.)* All right! Just listen to me for a moment! I am not taking—nor have I any intention of taking—either side in this issue—yet! He may be right and she may be just as right! But we have to settle this, and there's only one way to do it!

SIRELLI: And he's the one who suggested it! *(Indicating LAUDISI.)*

PREFECT: Really! Well, then! Let's hear it!

AGAZZI: Given that there is no factual proof, there remains only one thing to do. You must exercise your authority to obtain a statement from the wife.

PREFECT: From Signora Ponza?

SIRELLI: Without the presence of her husband, of course!

AGAZZI: Which will allow her to tell the truth!

SIRELLI: That she's the old lady's daughter, as we all believe her to be . . .

AGAZZI: . . . or else that she's Signor Ponza's second wife, obligingly playing the part of the daughter, as *he* says . . .

PREFECT: . . . and as I believe myself with no reservations! But, yes, I agree! There seems to be only one way. Believe me, that poor man wants nothing better than to prove that he's right. He's shown himself to be agreeable to everything I brought up to him. He'd be the most pleased of all, and you, my friends, could put your minds at rest.—Centuri, would you do me a favor? *(CENTURI rises.)* Fetch Signor Ponza for me from next door. Ask him if he wouldn't mind coming here for a moment. Tell him I'd be grateful.

CENTURI: I'll go at once! *(He bows and leaves by the rear door.)*

AGAZZI: I only hope he agrees!

PREFECT: He won't even hesitate. You'll see! A quarter of an hour, and it will be settled! Here, right here, in front of your very eyes!

AGAZZI: What? Here? In my house?

SIRELLI: Will he want to bring his wife here, do you think?

PREFECT: Leave it to me! Yes, I'll see her—and right here, too! Otherwise you people will never get over the idea that somehow I . . .

AGAZZI: Oh, but what nonsense!

SIRELLI: It would never occur to us!

PREFECT: Now, now! Since there's no doubt about how I feel, that he's in the right, and all that, you'd always suspect that since he's a public servant I might want to hush up the whole affair. But no . . . I want you all to be here to hear what's said. *(To AGAZZI.)* Your wife?

AGAZZI: In there—with some other ladies . . .

PREFECT: Looks to me like you've established a real conspirators' den!

CENTURI: *(Enters.)* Excuse me. Signor Ponza is here.

PREFECT: Thank you, Centuri. *(PONZA appears in the doorway.)* Do come in, my dear Ponza. Step inside.

(PONZA bows.)

AGAZZI: And make yourself comfortable.

(PONZA bows again and sits.)

PREFECT: I believe you know these gentlemen. Signor Sirelli . . .

(PONZA rises and bows.)

AGAZZI: Yes, of course, I've already introduced them. My brother-in law Laudisi.

(PONZA bows again.)

PREFECT: I've sent for you here, my good man, to let you know that I and these friends of mine . . . *(He interrupts himself when he notices that PONZA has grown very nervous and agitated from the time he first started talking.)* Is there anything you'd care to say . . . ?

PONZA: Yes, Signore. That I intend to submit an immediate request for transfer.

PREFECT: But why do a thing like that? Just a while ago you spoke to me with such patient understanding.

PONZA: I have been made the target, Signore, of unheard of persecution.

PREFECT: Oh, come now! Let's not exaggerate!

AGAZZI: *(To PONZA.)* Persecution, you said . . . did you mean me?

PONZA: Everyone! And that's why I'm leaving. *(To the PREFECT.)* I'm leaving, Signore, because this heartless, unrelenting inquisition into my private life has gone too far. In the end it will damage and finally destroy the work of charity I do that has cost me so much effort and so many sacrifices. I couldn't love that old lady more if she were my own mother. But yesterday, here, in this room, I was forced to treat her in the cruelest and most horrible way possible. And just now, over there, I found her in such a state of dejection and agitation that . . .

AGAZZI: *(Interrupting, calm.)* How strange! Because the Signora has always spoken to us in a very calm manner. On the contrary, Signor Ponza, the only agitation we have witnessed has come solely from you—and here we see it again.

PONZA: Because not one of you has any idea what you're making me suffer!

PREFECT: Calm yourself, my dear Ponza, calm yourself. What is it? After all, I'm here, and you know with what faith and sympathy I've listened to you. That's right, isn't it?

PONZA: Forgive me. Yes. It's true. And I'm grateful.

PREFECT: All right, then, listen. You say you love the poor woman as if she were your mother. Well, then, you should also realize that these friends of mine here are eaten up with curiosity because they're fond of the old lady, too.

PONZA: But they're killing her, Signore! I've told them about it more than once!

PREFECT: Just be patient. Once the matter is cleared up, it will all be over. And we'll do that now. It's simple. You have everything you need to remove any doubts in these people's minds. I, of course, have no doubts, as you know.

PONZA: No! They've made up their minds! They don't want to believe me!

AGAZZI: That's not true. When you came here following your mother-in-law's first visit and told us she was mad, we may have been surprised, but we believed you. *(To the PREFECT.)* Immediately after that, of course, the old lady returned, and . . .

PREFECT: Yes, yes, I know all that. You told me. *(Turning to PONZA, continuing.)* When she returned, she told the same story that you are trying to keep alive in her mind. It stands to reason that there will be certain distressing doubts in the mind of anyone who first hears your story and then hers. And so, my dear Ponza, you must understand that, considering what your mother-in-law has to say, these people can no longer accept what you say with total certainty. It's clear what we must do. You and your mother-in-law . . . out of the picture—simply step aside for the moment! Since you are as sure as I am that you're telling the truth, I can't imagine your objection to hearing it confirmed by the only person other than you and your mother-in-law who can possibly do so.

PONZA: And who is that?

PREFECT: Why, your wife, of course!

PONZA: My wife? *(Forcefully, with indignation.)* No, no! No, no! Never!

PREFECT: And may I ask why not?

PONZA: Bring my wife here for the satisfaction of those who don't believe me?

PREFECT: *(Quickly.)* No—for my satisfaction as well! Is there a problem?

PONZA: No—I beg of you—not my wife! No! She must be left out of this! You *have* to believe me!

PREFECT: Even to me, Signore, it's beginning to look like you're doing everything possible *not* to be believed!

AGAZZI: Especially considering he did everything possible to prevent his mother-in-law from coming here to speak. Not to mention the double insult to my wife and daughter.

PONZA: *(Bursting out, furiously.)* What in the name of God do you all want from me?! What?! Isn't my poor, unfortunate mother-in-law enough for you? You want to involve my wife in this, too? You want her to come here! I won't have it—I won't have this outrage! My wife stays where she is—at home! She will *not* be dragged out in front of *anyone!* *(To the PREFECT.)* It's enough to know that *you* believe me, Signore. And now I'll go fill out my request for transfer. *(He gets up.)*

PREFECT: *(Banging his fist on the table.)* Just one moment here, if you please! In the first place, you will *not* take that tone with your superior officer—nor with me! Especially considering the courtesy and understanding I have always shown you! In the second place—and I repeat—even I am beginning to have doubts about you! What else can I think when you stubbornly refuse to furnish me with the proof I have requested in your own interest? Which *I* requested, I repeat, and no one else! A request which appears to me to be utterly unobjectionable! There is no reason whatever why my colleague and I should not receive a visit from a lady . . . or, if you prefer, come to your home . . .

PONZA: Then you're really going to force me?

PREFECT: As I said before, it's for your own good. As your superior officer, I could order you.

PONZA: All right. All right. If that's the way it is, I'll bring my wife here, just to put an end to it! But how do I know that the poor old woman won't see her?

PREFECT: Yes, well . . . that's a point . . . considering she's just next door.

AGAZZI: *(Quickly.)* We could visit Signora Frola while you . . .

PONZA: No, no, not that! It's for you I say it. I want no more surprises from you, what with the horrible consequences they could bring!

AGAZZI: No need to worry about us.

PREFECT: Or if you prefer, you could bring her to my office at some convenient time..

PONZA: No, no—now—here—at once! When I get back, I'll go over and keep an eye on my mother-in-law. I'll go get her now, Signore, so that we can end this. Over—once and for all! *(He rushes out the door in the back wall.)*

PREFECT: I confess I didn't anticipate such resistance from him.

AGAZZI: You know what he's going to do, don't you? Tell his wife exactly what he wants her to say!

PREFECT: No, no! Don't worry your head about that. I'll be questioning the woman myself.

SIRELLI: I trust you noticed that his exasperation didn't lessen any.

PREFECT: Yes, well—it was the first time that I—mm—that I've seen him this way. Probably the thought of bringing his wife here—

SIRELLI: —releasing her from jail is more like it—

PREFECT: —as for keeping her like she was a prisoner—that can be explained without assuming that he's mad.

SIRELLI: You'll excuse me, Prefect, but you haven't yet heard what the poor woman has to say.

AGAZZI: Yes! And he claims he keeps her shut up in fear of what his mother-in-law might do.

PREFECT: But even if that were not the case, he might still be jealous of her, and that would be quite enough.

SIRELLI: To the extent of not even providing her one single housemaid? His wife has to do all the housework!

AGAZZI: And he does all the shopping himself! Every morning!

CENTURI: That's true! I've seen him! Carries everything back with the help of a boy—

SIRELLI: —and the boy's not even allowed in the door!

PREFECT: But, good God, gentlemen! He complained about the nuisance himself when we spoke earlier!

LAUDISI: And he is certainly an irreproachable information service!

PREFECT: It's to save money, Laudisi! He has two households to maintain—

SIRELLI: But that's not why we're saying it! Does it seem likely to you that a second wife would take on such a burden—

AGAZZI: *(Growing angry.)* —the most menial household tasks—

SIRELLI: *(Continuing the speech.)* —for someone who was once her husband's mother-in-law and means nothing to her personally?

AGAZZI: I ask you now! Isn't that just a bit too much—

PREFECT: A bit too much, yes—

LAUDISI: *(Interrupting.)* —to believe of any ordinary second wife?

PREFECT: *(Quickly.)* Admittedly! Too much! Yes! But even this can be explained! If not by generosity, then by jealousy! And even though Ponza may or may not be mad—he is most certainly a jealous man!
(A confused clamor of voices is heard from the drawing room.)

AGAZZI: What's going on in there?

AMALIA: *(In a state of consternation, enters in great haste through the door at the left, announcing.)* Signora Frola! Signora Frola's here!

AGAZZI: Oh, no! For God's sake! Who sent for her?

AMALIA: No one! She came on her own!

PREFECT: No! For heaven's sake! Not now! Send her away, please, Signora!

AGAZZI: Yes, now, at once! Don't let her in! Keep her out no matter what! If he finds her here again, it's sure to look like a trap!
(SIGNORA FROLA enters trembling, weeping, beseeching, a handkerchief in her hand, and accompanied by an agitated crowd of people from the drawing room.)

SIGNORA FROLA: Gentlemen, oh, gentlemen, for pity's sake, please! Signor Agazzi, tell them! Tell everyone!

AGAZZI: *(Coming forward, very angry.)* Signora, I must insist that you leave here at once! We cannot allow you to stay here! Not now!

SIGNORA FROLA: *(Bewildered.)* But why? Why? *(To AMALIA.)* I beg you, dear, kind Signora!

AMALIA: Yes, but, you see . . . you see, Signora, the Prefect is here . . .

SIGNORA FROLA: The Prefect! Oh, Signore, have pity on me! I was coming to see you!

PREFECT: No, Signora, please, try to understand! I can't talk to you now. You'll have to go! Go at once!

SIGNORA FROLA: Yes, Prefect, all right, I'm going! I'll leave today! Right away! You'll never see me again!

AGAZZI: Now, now, Signora! We only want you to leave for a moment. Just go back into your apartment and wait. Would you do me this favor? Please! You can then speak to the Prefect.

SIGNORA FROLA: But why? What is it? What?

AGAZZI: *(Losing his patience.)* What it is is your son-in-law is about to arrive! Is that clear enough?

SIGNORA FROLA: Oh! Is he? Well, then, yes . . . yes, I'll go . . . I'll go at once! But there's one thing I wanted to tell you all. You must stop this! Out of pity for us! Stop what you're doing! You think you're helping, but what you're really doing me is great harm! I'll have no choice but to leave, leave now, if you continue! I'll leave this very day. At least he'll be left in peace! But what do you want with him now? Why do you want him here now? Why is he coming? Oh, Prefect!

PREFECT: It's nothing, Signora, nothing, don't worry, just step out, please, won't you?

AMALIA: Do come along now, Signora. Come, trust us.

SIGNORA FROLA: Oh, my God, Signora, they're taking from me the one remaining comfort I have in life: the pleasure of seeing my daughter, if only at a distance! *(She begins to weep.)*

PREFECT: Who told you such a thing? Nor is there any reason to leave town! We only asked you to leave us for a moment. You're not to worry.

SIGNORA FROLA: But I *do* worry! I worry about *him!* I came here to beg you all in his name! I came for *him, not* myself!

PREFECT: Yes, all right. And you're not to worry about him either. I assure you. You'll see. The whole matter will be cleared up once and for all.

SIGNORA FROLA: But how? All I see is that everyone here is out to get him!

PREFECT: No, Signora! That's not true! I'm here to help him if he needs it. So don't worry!

SIGNORA FROLA: Oh, thank you! At least I know you understand!

PREFECT: Of course, Signora, of course I understand . . .

SIGNORA FROLA: I've told these ladies and gentlemen so many times that it was a misfortune in the past, but it's over now and must be left there!

PREFECT: I understand! Yes, Signora! I assure you!

SIGNORA FROLA: We're happy to live like this, both of us. My daughter is happy. And so . . . See to it, please, please, because if you don't there's only one choice left for me, and that is to leave here and never see her again! Not even from a long way off . . . the way I do now . . . So for pity's sake, leave him in peace!

(A movement in the crowd becomes noticeable; some make gestures, while others look at the door. Several voices are heard speaking in an undertone.)

VOICES: Oh, God! . . . There she is! . . . There she is!

SIGNORA FROLA: *(Noticing the general dismay and uneasiness in the gathering groans, perplexed and trembling.)* What is it? What's happening?

(Everyone in the room parts to one side or the other to make way for SIGNORA PONZA who enters and comes forward rigidly. She is dressed in mourning, her face covered by a thick, black, impenetrable veil.)

SIGNORA FROLA: *(With a piercing cry of frantic joy.)* Oh! Lina! Lina! Lina!

(She rushes forward and throws her arms around the veiled figure with the passion of a mother who has not embraced her daughter for many years. At the same time, from outside the room, the voice of PONZA is heard and he rushes into the room.)

SIGNOR PONZA: *(From outside.)* Julia! Julia! Julia! (At the sound of PONZA's cry, SIGNORA PONZA's body goes visibly rigid in SIGNORA FROLA's embrace. Rushing in, PONZA suddenly sees his mother-in-law totally lost in her embrace of his wife and cries out in a furious rage.)* Ah! I knew it! Cowards! Taking advantage of my good faith!

SIGNORA PONZA: *(Turning her veiled face to him with austere solemnity.)* Don't be afraid! Don't be afraid! Go now.

PONZA: *(Softly, lovingly, to SIGNORA FROLA.)* Let's go, yes, let's go . . .

SIGNORA FROLA: *(Trembling and humble, releases her embrace and immediately echoes PONZA's words in her concern for him.)* Yes, yes . . . let's go, my dear, let's go . . .

(Their arms around each other, exchanging affectionate caresses, and crying each in their own way, the two of them go out whispering endearments to each other. Silence. Bewildered and touched at the same time, all present,

who have kept their eyes on the couple as they made their way out, now turn their attention to the veiled figure.)

SIGNORA PONZA: *(Having observed them through her veil, now speaks to them with dark solemnity.)* Ladies and gentlemen, after this, what more can you ask of me? As you see, we have a misfortune here that must remain hidden; a misfortune for which there is only one remedy; and that remedy is the compassion already provided by family love and duty.

PREFECT: *(Moved.)* And we insist on respecting that love and duty, Signora.—And yet, what we would like you to tell us . . .

SIGNORA PONZA: *(Speaking slowly and with great clarity.)* . . . is what? The truth? The truth is this. That I am—yes—the daughter of Signora Frola—

ALL: *(With a sigh of satisfaction.)* Ah!

SIGNORA PONZA: *(As above.)* —and Signor Ponza's second wife—

ALL: *(Stunned and disappointed, subdued.)* Oh!—But how?

SIGNORA PONZA: *(At once, as above.)* —yes; and for myself I am no one! No one!

PREFECT: No, Signora, no! For yourself you must be either one or the other!

SIGNORA PONZA: No. Not at all. I am the one you believe me to be. *(She looks at everyone through her veil for a moment and goes out. Silence.)*

LAUDISI: So there you have it, ladies and gentlemen! The voice of truth! *(Looking around him in mocking defiance.)* Are you happy now? *(Bursts out laughing.)* Ha-ha-ha-ha!

END OF PLAY

Six Characters in Search of an Author

(Sei personaggi in cerca d'autore)

1921

CAST OF CHARACTERS

CHARACTERS IN THE PLAY IN THE MAKING
The Father
The Mother
The Stepdaughter
The Son
The Boy *non-speaking rôle*
The Little Girl *non-speaking rôle*
Madame Pace *who is later summoned into being*

THE COMPANY
The Director
The Female Lead
The Male Lead
The Second Female Lead
The Ingenue
The Juvenile Lead
Other Actors
The Stage Manager
The Prompter
The Property Man
The Crew Head
The Stage Door Attendant
Stagehands and Other Backstage Workers

TIME AND PLACE

Daytime. The stage of a theater.

Six Characters in Search of an Author

ACT ONE

The audience enters to see the curtain raised and the stage looking as it does during the day. There are neither wings nor sets; the stage is empty and nearly dark; the immediate impression being that the audience will not be seeing a rehearsed play but a performance that suddenly materializes. Two small flights of steps, right and left, lead from the auditorium to the stage. The prompter's box cover has been removed and sits beside the opening. Downstage on the opposite side are a small table and an armchair with its back to the audience. It is for the Director. Two additional small tables, one larger, one smaller, along with several chairs, have been set up downstage in case they are needed for the rehearsal. Other chairs, right and left, are for the actors. There is a piano upstage and to the side that is almost hidden. When the lights in the auditorium have gone down, the CREW HEAD, dressed in dark blue work clothes and with a bag of tools hung from his belt, enters through a door. He takes a couple of boards from an upstage corner, brings them downstage, kneels, and begins to nail them together. At the sound of the hammer blows, the STAGE MANAGER rushes in through the door leading to the dressing rooms.

STAGE MANAGER: What the hell's going on out here!

CREW HEAD: What's it look like? Nailing!

STAGE MANAGER: *(Looking at his watch.)* It's 10:30! Rehearsal's about to begin. The director's due any minute.

CREW HEAD: So when do I work?

STAGE MANAGER: Anytime. Just not now.

CREW HEAD: When?

STAGE MANAGER: When we're done. Okay? Get this stuff out of here. I need to set up. Second act. *Rules of the Game.*
(The CREW HEAD grumbles as he clears away the wood and tools and goes off. Meanwhile the COMPANY OF ACTORS enters through a door upstage,

singly at first, then in groups of two or three, as they choose. Altogether there are nine or ten, as many as are required for today's rehearsal of Pirandello's The Rules of the Game. *On entering, they greet one another and the STAGE MANAGER. Some go off to their dressing rooms; others, the PROMPTER, with the prompt script rolled up under his arm, among them, await the Director. Some stand, others sit, passing the time of day. One lights a cigarette, another complains about the rôle he's been assigned, and a third reads aloud from a theatrical journal for the benefit of his colleagues. Ideally, the ACTORS should be dressed in bright, happy colors in order that this first, improvised scene be played with great natural vivacity. Sometime or other an ACTOR goes to the piano, sits, and plays while several of the younger ACTORS begin to dance to the music.)*

STAGE MANAGER: *(Clapping his hands to get their attention.)* Okay! Get a move on! Let's go! The boss just arrived!

(The music and dancing stop suddenly. The ACTORS look out into the auditorium at the DIRECTOR who has entered through the rear door. His clothes reveal that he is a man of substance. He walks the entire length of the auditorium and climbs up one of the short flights of steps leading onto the stage. The ACTORS greet him as he approaches. The PROMPTER hands him his mail—several newspapers and a manuscript.)

DIRECTOR. No letters?

PROMPTER. This is it, sir.

DIRECTOR: *(Handing him back the manuscript.)* Put them in my office. *(Looks around; to the STAGE MANAGER.)* How about some light? Can't see a thing out here.

PROMPTER: Right away, sir. *(He gives the order and almost at once the right side of the stage where the ACTORS are standing is illuminated by a harsh, bright light. The PROMPTER has taken his seat with the prompt script in front of him.)*

DIRECTOR: *(Clapping his hands.)* All right! Let's get started! *(To the STAGE MANAGER.)* Anyone missing?

STAGE MANAGER: Miss You-know-who hasn't arrived yet.

DIRECTOR: As usual. *(Looks at his watch.)* Ten minutes late already. Remind me to talk to her. We begin on time. *(He has scarcely finished speaking when the voice of the FEMALE LEAD is heard from the auditorium.)*

FEMALE LEAD: Come on! Have a heart! I'm here! *(She is dressed entirely in white, wears a large, extravagant hat, and carries a small dog on her arm. She runs down the aisle and hurries up the steps to the stage.)*

DIRECTOR: I take it you enjoy making us wait?

FEMALE LEAD: Sorry. Couldn't find a taxi. You haven't even started. Besides, I'm not on in the first scene. *(Then, calling the STAGE MANAGER by name, she hands him the dog.)* Be an angel. Put him in my dressing room and shut the door?

DIRECTOR: One dog more or less. *(Claps his hands again; to the PROMPTER.)* Okay! Let's get on with it! Second act! *Rules of the Game.* Let's go! *(He sits in his armchair.)* Clear the stage! Who's on?

(The ACTORS clear off of the stage and take seats at either side, except for the three who begin the scene, and the FEMALE LEAD who has paid no attention to the DIRECTOR and has sat down at one of the small tables.)

DIRECTOR: *(To the FEMALE LEAD.)* Am I to understand that you are now in this scene, madam?

FEMALE LEAD: Who? Me? No.

DIRECTOR: *(Exasperated.)* Then for Christ's sake would you kindly vacate your post? Go! Please! *(She rises and takes a seat with the others. To the PROMPTER.)* Can we get started!

PROMPTER: *(Reads from the script.)* "The house of Leone Gala. An unusual room, serving as both dining room and study."

DIRECTOR: *(To the STAGE MANAGER.)* Let's have the red set.

STAGE MANAGER: *(Taking a note).* Red set. Right.

PROMPTER: *(Continues reading.)* "A table set for dinner and a desk piled with books and papers. Bookshelves. Glass-doored cupboards containing valuable china. Upstage, the door to Leone's bedroom. To the left, a door to the kitchen. Main entrance, right."

DIRECTOR: *(Rising and pointing.)* All right! Pay attention! Main entrance, there. Door to kitchen, here. *(To the ACTOR playing the rôle of Socrates.)* You enter and exit from here. *(To the STAGE MANAGER.)* Let's have a screen upstage and some curtains. *(He sits.)*

STAGE MANAGER: *(Taking a note).* Got it.

PROMPTER: *(Reading.)* "Scene One. Leone Gala, Guido Venenzi, Filippo, known as Socrates." *(To the DIRECTOR.)* Should I read the stage directions?

DIRECTOR: For the hundredth time—yes!

PROMPTER: *(Reading.)* "At rise, Leone Gala, wearing a cook's hat and apron, is beating an egg in a bowl with a wooden spoon. Filippo, also dressed as a cook, beats another egg. Guido Venanzi sits and listens to them."

MALE LEAD: *(To the DIRECTOR.)* Do I have to wear this stupid hat?

DIRECTOR: *(Annoyed.)* That's what it says here, that's what you wear. *(He indicates the manuscript.)*

MALE LEAD: But it's ridiculous.

DIRECTOR: *(Jumping up in a rage.)* Ridiculous? Is it my fault plays are crap these days? Is it my fault we're reduced to reviving Pirandello, for God's sake, understood by no one, whether public or critic! *(The ACTORS laugh. The DIRECTOR goes to the MALE LEAD and shouts.)* So, yes! You wear the stupid hat! You beat the stupid eggs! And once you've got that down, you can start acting the shells of the eggs that you're beating! *(The ACTORS laugh again and make ironic comments to each other.)* Shut up! Listen to me when I talk! *(To the MALE LEAD.)* That's right! The shells! The shell of the egg is the empty form of reason! Its contents are instinct! Which is blind! You are reason! Your wife is instinct! Each of you is incomplete! You each play the rôle assigned to you in the game! And when you play those rôles, you are each playing the puppet representation of yourself! Understand?

MALE LEAD: No.

DIRECTOR: *(Returns to his seat.)* Neither do I. Can we get on with this? What a disaster! And please speak up. If the audience can't hear, we might as well not waste our time.

(Meanwhile the STAGE DOOR ATTENDANT, wearing a cap, has entered the auditorium from the rear, and comes all the way down the aisle to the edge of the stage to announce the arrival of the SIX CHARACTERS. They have followed him at a short distance. They look around, a bit perplexed and dismayed. It is imperative that the SIX CHARACTERS not be confused with the ACTORS onstage. The placement of the two groups, as described in stage directions, will undoubtedly help, as well as their being lit in different colors. But the most effective and suitable means of distinguishing them will be the use of special masks for the SIX CHARACTERS. These masks must be made of material that will not go limp with perspiration, but which at the same time are light enough for the actors to wear. The eyes, nose, and mouth must remain free. This will help to emphasize the profound significance of the play. The SIX CHARACTERS must never appear as phantasms, but as created realities, unchangeable creations of the imagination, and thus more real and more consistent than the inconsistent naturalness of the ACTORS. The masks will also help give the impression of figures constructed by art, each one fixed immutably in the expression of the sentiment fundamental to it: Remorse for the FATHER, Revenge for the STEPDAUGHTER, Sorrow for the MOTHER, whose mask must have wax tears

in the corners of the eyes and down the cheeks, as on statues and in pictures of the Mater Dolorosa to be seen in churches. Even her dress should be made of a special material and cut, extremely plain, with severe folds, looking as if it had been carved. In any case, it must not give the impression that it is made of a material that one can buy anywhere or that just any dressmaker can construct. The FATHER is around fifty, with reddish hair, thinning at the temples. He wears a thick mustache over his still youthful mouth that often falls open in an empty and uncertain smile. He is pale, with a broad brow and blue piercing eyes that are an oval shape. He wears a dark jacket and light trousers. His manner is at times sweet, while at other times hard and harsh. The MOTHER is a woman who is crushed and terrified by an intolerable weight of shame and abasement. She is dressed in modest black and wears a thick crepe widow's veil. When she lifts the veil, she reveals a wax-like face. Her eyes are always downcast. The STEPDAUGHTER is eighteen, beautiful, dashing, and almost impudent. She, too, is dressed in mourning, but wears it with somewhat gaudy elegance. She shows contempt for her frightened, dejected, fourteen-year-old, younger brother. He is grubby and also dressed in black. On the other hand, she displays a lively tenderness for her sister, the LITTLE GIRL, who is about four years old and wears a white dress with a black silk sash at the waist. The SON is a tall, severe, twenty-two-year-old. He shows contempt for his father and supercilious indifference toward his mother. He is dressed properly but is obviously not in mourning.)

STAGE DOOR ATTENDANT: *(Cap in hand.)* Excuse me, sir.

DIRECTOR: *(Rudely.)* What do you want now!

STAGE DOOR ATTENDANT: *(Timidly.)* Some people, sir. Asking for you. *(The DIRECTOR and the ACTORS turn in astonishment and look out into the auditorium.)*

DIRECTOR: *(Furiously.)* Goddamn it! I'm rehearsing! Rehearsals are *closed! (To the SIX CHARACTERS.)* Who are you? What do you want?

FATHER: *(Comes forward to the foot of one of the flights of steps; the others follow.)* We're in search of an author.

DIRECTOR: *(Between anger and astonishment.)* An author? What author?

FATHER: Any author, sir.

DIRECTOR: There's no author here! We're not doing a new play.

STEPDAUGHTER: *(Vivaciously as she rushes up the steps.)* All the better, sir. Then we can be your new play.

AN ACTOR: *(As the other ACTORS make lively comments and laugh.)* That has to be a first!

FATHER: *(Following the STEPDAUGHTER onto the stage.)* Yes, but—if there's no author . . . *(To the DIRECTOR.)* then perhaps you could be the author . . .
(The MOTHER, holding the LITTLE GIRL by the hand, and followed by the BOY, climbs the first steps to the stage.)

DIRECTOR: Is this some kind of joke?

FATHER: But, sir, how can you say that? On the contrary, the play we offer you is one of terrible sadness.

STEPDAUGHTER: We might even make you a fortune.

DIRECTOR: Do me a favor. Disappear. We're not equipped to deal with lunatics.

FATHER: *(Hurt, but gently.)* But as you must know, sir, life is full of absurdities that have no need to masquerade as truth. Just because they *are* true.

DIRECTOR: What the hell are you talking about?

FATHER: I'm saying that, to reverse the order of things, to pretend that what is *not* real *is* real, may well be considered insanity. But this insanity is the very basis of your profession.
(The ACTORS become nervous and offended.)

DIRECTOR: *(Rises and looks him up and down.)* Which makes *us* a bunch of lunatics?

FATHER: I mean—making what *isn't* true *seem* true. Without having to. Just for fun. Isn't the aim of your profession to give life to imaginary characters on the stage?

DIRECTOR: *(Immediately; interpreting the rising anger of the company.)* Let me advise you, sir. The actor's profession is a noble one. If today's playwrights give us nothing but stupid comedies to act and puppets to play instead of human beings—at least we can claim that we have given life on this stage to immortal works.
(The ACTORS nod approval and applaud.)

FATHER: *(Interrupting; passionately.)* Yes. Exactly! To beings more alive than those who breathe and wear clothes! Less real, but truer! I agree with you! Entirely!
(The ACTORS look at each other in astonishment.)

DIRECTOR: Oh, come on! You just said . . .

FATHER: No. I'm sorry, sir. I'm sorry. I only said that for your sake. You screamed at us. You had no time for lunatics. You especially should know that nature reaches her highest creative level through imagination.

DIRECTOR: Fine! Fine! What are you trying to say?

FATHER: Nothing. Just to show you that one can be born in many different forms. A tree. A stone. Water. Butterfly. A woman. Even as a character for the stage.

DIRECTOR: *(Ironically, with feigned amazement.)* And you and your friends here were born as . . . characters for the stage?

FATHER: Exactly. And alive. As you can see. *(The DIRECTOR and the ACTORS burst out laughing. Father is hurt.)* I'm sorry we make you laugh. As I said, we carry in us a drama of terrible sadness. As you can surmise from this woman veiled in black.

(And having said this, he holds out his hand to help the MOTHER up the last few steps onto the stage. He leads her with a kind of tragic solemnity to the other side that is immediately illuminated in a fantastic kind of light. The LITTLE GIRL and the BOY follow their MOTHER. The SON comes up next and takes a place to one side in the rear. Finally the STEP-DAUGHTER comes up and leans against the proscenium. The ACTORS, at first astonished at the proceedings, are caught up in admiration of this development and burst into applause as if at a performance.)

DIRECTOR: *(First astonished, then indignant.)* All right! That's enough! Quiet! *(To the SIX CHARACTERS.)* I want you out of here! Off this stage! *Now! (To the STAGE MANAGER.)* Get them out!

STAGE MANAGER: *(Comes forward and then stops as if held back by some strange fear.)* Come on! Let's go! Out!

FATHER: *(To the DIRECTOR.)* No! No! You don't. . . we . . .

DIRECTOR: *(Shouting.)* We have work to do!

MALE LEAD: And we don't like being made fools of!

FATHER: *(Coming forward with determination.)* I don't understand. Aren't you used to seeing an author's characters spring to life on stage? Just because we have no script here—*(He indicates the PROMPTER who holds the production book.)* with us as characters . . .

STEPDAUGHTER: *(Approaches the DIRECTOR, smiling and seductive).* Sir. We really are six very interesting characters. But we have nowhere to go.

FATHER: *(Brushes her aside.)* That's it. *(To the DIRECTOR without pausing.)* The author who gave us life either didn't want to, or couldn't put us into a work of art. That's a crime. Because if you're fortunate enough to be born a living character you can laugh even at death. You can't die. The man, the writer, the instrument of your creation, will die. But his creation will never die. And to live forever as a character you don't have to be talented or able to work miracles. Who was Don Quixote? Who was

Sancho Panza? And yet they live forever. They were seeds that found a womb. An imagination to raise and nourish them. To make them eternal.

DIRECTOR: Fine. But what do you want here?

FATHER: To live, sir.

DIRECTOR: *(Ironically.)* For ever and ever?

FATHER: No, sir. Only for a moment. In them.

AN ACTOR: Oh, God!

FEMALE LEAD: They want to live! In us!

YOUNG ACTOR: *(Indicating the STEPDAUGHTER.)* Great! As long as I get *her!*

FATHER: No! Listen! Please! The play still has to be made. *(To the DIRECTOR.)* If you and your actors are ready, we can get started.

DIRECTOR *(Annoyed.)* What is it you want to get started on? We don't do that kind of thing here. We put on regular plays.

FATHER: Exactly. That's why we came.

DIRECTOR: Then where's the script?

FATHER: In us, sir. *(The ACTORS laugh.)* The play is in us. We are the play. It's our passion drives us to this.

STEPDAUGHTER: *(Scornful and alluring, treacherous, impudent.)* If only you knew *my* passion, sir. My passion for *him*. *(She indicates the FATHER and pretends as if to embrace him, then bursts into wild laughter.)*

FATHER: *(Breaks into a rage.)* Keep out of this! Behave yourself! And don't laugh like that!

STEPDAUGHTER: Really? With your permission, ladies and gentlemen. Though I lost my father only two months ago, I would like to do a little song-and-dance number for you. *(She mischievously starts to sing Dave Stamper's "Prend garde à Tchou-Tchin-Tchou" in the fox-trot or slow one-step version arranged by François Salabert. She sings the first verse as she accompanies it with a dance.)*

> Les chinois sont un peuple malin,
> De Shangaï à Pekin,
> Ils ont mis des écriteaux partout:
> Prenez garde à Tchou-Tchin-Tchou!

(While she is singing and dancing, the ACTORS, especially the younger ones, move toward her as if attracted by some strange fascination, and raise their hands slightly as if to grasp her. She slips away, and when the ACTORS applaud and the DIRECTOR scolds her, she stands unmoving, abstractedly, as if a long way off.)

THE ACTORS: *(Laughing and clapping.)* Bravo! Well done! Great!

DIRECTOR: *(Irately.)* Shut up! This is not a cabaret! *(Pulling the FATHER aside; in consternation.)* Is she insane?

FATHER: Insane? No! Worse!

STEPDAUGHTER: *(Running to the DIRECTOR.)* Worse! Worse! Much, much worse! Please! We must get this play on as soon as possible. Then you'll see that at a certain moment I'll run away. I'll run away when this dear sweet child . . . *(She takes the LITTLE GIRL standing by the MOTHER by the hand and leads her over to the DIRECTOR.)* Isn't she sweet? *(Takes her in her arms and kisses her.)* Oh, my dear, my sweet! *(Puts her down and continues emotionally, almost against her will.)* When God suddenly takes this dear little thing away from her mother, and when that idiot there *(Grabs hold of the BOY by his arm and roughly drags him forward.)* does the stupidest things, like the fool he is. *(Pushes him back toward the MOTHER.)* Then you'll see me run away. Oh, and how I long for that moment. Because after all the intimate things that have happened between me and him . . . *(With a horrible wink at the FATHER.)* I can't stay with these people any longer, can't bear to see my mother's anguish over that fool . . . *(Indicates the SON.)* Look at him! Look at him! How cold and indifferent he is. Just because he's the legitimate son. Him! He despises me. Despises *him. (Indicates the BOY.)* That poor little creature. Because we're bastards. Do you understand? Bastards. *(She goes over to the MOTHER and embraces her.)* And this poor woman, here, the mother of us all, he refuses to recognize as his mother! Because she's also the mother of us three bastards. *(To the SON.)* You're vile! *(She says all this very rapidly and with great emotional distress. "Bastards" is said very loudly, and the word* vile *is spoken in a very low voice as if she were spitting it out.)*

MOTHER: *(With great anguish; to the DIRECTOR.)* Please! I beg you! In the name of these two little children! *(She is faint and about to fall.)* Oh, God . . . *(The ACTORS are dismayed and bewildered.)*

FATHER: *(Rushing to her aid.)* Please! A chair! A chair for this poor widow!

ACTORS: *(Hurry over to her.)* Is she all right? Has she fainted?

DIRECTOR: Hurry! Bring a chair!

(An ACTOR brings a chair. The others surround her, trying to help. The MOTHER has sat down and tries to prevent the FATHER from lifting her veil.)

FATHER: Look at her, sir. Look at her . . .

MOTHER: No! No! My God! Don't!

FATHER: Let them see you! *(He lifts the veil.)*

MOTHER: *(Rises in desperation and covers her face with her hands.)* Please, sir! Don't let this man carry out his plan! It's horrible!

DIRECTOR: *(Dumbfounded.)* I'm afraid I don't understand this. What's going on? *(To the FATHER.)* Is she your wife?

FATHER: *(Quickly.)* Yes, sir. My wife.

DIRECTOR: Then how can she be a widow? You're still alive.

(The ACTORS relieve their bewilderment with loud laughter.)

FATHER: *(Hurt, with resentment.)* Don't laugh! Don't laugh like that! This is her tragedy, sir. She had a lover. Another man. Who ought to be here.

MOTHER: *(With a cry.)* No! No!

STEPDAUGHTER: He's lucky to be dead. He died two months ago. We're still in mourning.

FATHER: It's not because he's dead that he isn't here. He's not here because . . . well, look at her, sir. You'll understand. Her tragedy isn't that of a woman who loved two men. She was incapable of love. She felt nothing. At least no more than gratitude. For him. Not for me. She's not a woman. She's a mother. And her tragedy, sir—which I assure you is very powerful— consists in these four children she had with two men.

MOTHER: *I* had them? How dare you! *I* had these two men? I never even wanted them! He's the one! He's the one who forced him on me! He's the one who forced me to go away with him!

STEPDAUGHTER: *(Indignant.)* Not true!

MOTHER: *(Startled.)* What do you mean not true!

STEPDAUGHTER: Not true! Not true!

MOTHER: What do you know about it!

STEPDAUGHTER: It's not true! *(To the DIRECTOR.)* Don't believe her. Do you know why she said it? Because of him. *(Indicates the SON.)* That's why she said it. Because she tortures herself. Exhausts herself with anguish. Because her son rejects her. She wants him to understand that if she abandoned him when he was two years old, it was because he . . . *(Indicates the FATHER.)* he forced her to do it!

MOTHER: *(Forcefully.)* He forced me! He forced me! God is my witness! *(To the DIRECTOR.)* Ask him! *(Indicates her HUSBAND.)* Ask him if it's true! Let *him* tell my son! She *(Indicates the STEPDAUGHTER.)* knows nothing about it!

STEPDAUGHTER: I know that while my father was alive you had a peaceful and happy life with him. You can't deny that.

MOTHER: No. I don't deny it.

STEPDAUGHTER: And he was always loving to you. Kind. *(Angrily, to the BOY.)* It's true! Say so, you stupid little idiot! Say it!

MOTHER: Leave him alone! Why must you make me appear ungrateful? I don't want to offend your father. All I said was that it wasn't my fault. That it wasn't to satisfy my own desires that I abandoned my house and my son.

FATHER: It's true, sir. It was my fault.

(Pause.)

MALE LEAD: *(To the other ACTORS.)* Not bad!

FEMALE LEAD: Beats rehearsing.

YOUNG ACTOR: Wow!

DIRECTOR: *(Beginning to show a lively interest.)* Listen to them! Let's hear them out! *(Having said this, he descends one of the step units into the auditorium to gain an audience's perspective.)*

SON: *(Without moving from his position, coldly, softly, ironically.)* Ah! Here comes the philosophy! We will now hear about the Demon of Proof!

FATHER: Cynical idiot! *(To the DIRECTOR.)* He mocks me because I have a habit of defending myself.

SON: *(Scornfully.)* Words!

FATHER: Words! Yes! Words! A single word brings comfort when faced with the inexplicable. Or when pursued by an evil that destroys us. A word, a single word, that brings no answers, can bring us peace.

STEPDAUGHTER: Even where remorse is concerned. Especially there.

FATHER: Remorse? No. It took more than words to quiet that.

STEPDAUGHTER: Money? Yes. Money. The hundred lire he offered me in payment, ladies and gentlemen.

(The ACTORS are shocked.)

SON: *(Contemptuously to the STEPDAUGHTER.)* That was vile!

STEPDAUGHTER: Vile? But there they were. In a light blue envelope. On a little mahogany table. In a room behind Madame Pace's shop. *(To the DIRECTOR.)* Understand? Madame Pace. A woman who attracts poor girls from good families into her shop. Under the pretext of selling coats and dresses.

SON: And with it she bought the right to tyrannize over us all. That's what she's done. With the hundred lire that he never got the chance to pay her, and which—and you will note this—he had no reason to.

STEPDAUGHTER: Ah, but it was so close. So close. We almost did it. *(A burst of loud laughter.)*

MOTHER: *(Protesting.)* You should be ashamed.

STEPDAUGHTER: Ashamed? It's my revenge. I'm dying to play that scene. Dying to play it. The room. The wardrobe with the glass doors. The coats inside. The divan. Over there. The long mirror. The screen. And in front of the window the little mahogany table. With the light blue envelope. And the hundred lire inside. I see it so clearly. I could reach out. Take it in my hand. But you gentlemen will have to turn your backs. I'm nearly naked. No. I don't blush anymore. I leave that to him. *(Indicates the FATHER.)* But I assure you. He was very pale at the time. Very pale. *(To the DIRECTOR.)* Believe me.

DIRECTOR: What the hell is going on here!

FATHER: What's going on? She's assaulting you. Get some order here and let me speak. Don't believe all the slanders she's hurled at me. Give me a chance to explain.

STEPDAUGHTER: I've heard enough fairy tales!

FATHER: No fairy tales! Explanations!

STEPDAUGHTER: And all in your favor, no doubt.

(The DIRECTOR comes back on stage to restore order.)

FATHER: Don't you see! This is the cause of our trouble. We each have a world inside of us. Each his own world. So how can we understand each other? I put in my words the sense and meaning of things as I understand them in my world. And you, hearing those words, assume them to have the sense and meaning you put on them in your world. We think we understand each other. But we never do. Consider the pity, the utter pity I feel for this woman. *(Indicates the MOTHER.)* Which she sees as ferocious cruelty.

MOTHER: But you drove me out of the house.

FATHER: You see? Drove her out. She actually believed I drove her out.

MOTHER: You know how to talk. I don't. But believe me, sir—after he married me—and who knows why—I became a poor insignificant woman.

FATHER: I married you for your humility. I loved you for it, believing . . .

(He stops when he sees her making signs to contradict him, and turning to the DIRECTOR, opens his arms wide in a gesture of despair over not making himself understood.) You see? No. It's terrifying. Believe me. *(Taps his head.)* This mental deafness of hers is terrifying. Heart? Oh, yes. For the children. But deaf. Mentally deaf. Deaf to the point of desperation.

STEPDAUGHTER: True. But ask him what use his intelligence was to us.

FATHER: We think we do good, and we do evil. Thank God we don't realize it.

(The FEMALE LEAD has been growing steadily furious at seeing the

MALE LEAD *flirting with the STEPDAUGHTER. She now comes forward to the DIRECTOR.)*

FEMALE LEAD: Excuse me. Are we rehearsing today?

DIRECTOR: Yes, of course. But first I want to listen.

YOUNG ACTOR: I've never seen anything like this.

INGENUE: It's fascinating.

FEMALE LEAD: If you happen to like this sort of thing. *(She throws a glance at the MALE LEAD.)*

DIRECTOR: *(To the FATHER.)* Just be as clear as you can. *(He sits.)*

FATHER: I will. Well—you see, sir—I had a man working for me—a poor man—my secretary. He was devoted to me. And he understood her *(Indicates the MOTHER.)* in every way. They were kindred souls. Humble. Both of them incapable of doing any evil. Or even thinking it.

STEPDAUGHTER: So he thought of it for them. And went out and did it.

FATHER: That's not true. I wanted the best for both of them. And for myself. I confess. But I couldn't say a word without a quick glance passing between them. How to understand me. How not to anger me. I couldn't stand it. It was unendurable.

DIRECTOR: Why didn't you get rid of him?

FATHER: Yes. That's what I did. And then I watched her drag around the house like some lost creature. Some animal you've taken in out of pity.

MOTHER: Ah, yes . . .

FATHER: *(Turning quickly toward her as if to prevent her from speaking.)* Your son! You were going to tell him about your son! Weren't you?

MOTHER: First he tore my son away from me.

FATHER: But not for cruelty's sake. I wanted him to grow up—sound and healthy—in the country.

STEPDAUGHTER: *(Ironically; indicating the SON.)* Behold the results.

FATHER: *(Quickly.)* Is it my fault he turned out this way? I sent him to a wet-nurse in the country. A peasant's wife. She *(Indicates the MOTHER.)* wasn't strong enough, even though she'd come from the same humble surroundings. The reason I married her in the first place. Stupid? Maybe. But what could I do? I've always had this insane desire for moral healthiness. *(The STEPDAUGHTER bursts into loud laughter.)* Stop that! I can't stand it!

DIRECTOR: Quiet! I'm trying to listen. *(At the DIRECTOR's reprimand, she immediately returns to her former attitude, absorbed and distant, a half-smile on her lips. The DIRECTOR goes back into the auditorium in order to get an audience perspective.)*

FATHER: I couldn't bear seeing that woman any longer. *(Indicates the MOTHER.)* Not just because she bored me. But the nausea, the real nausea that came from the pity I felt for her.

MOTHER: So he sent me away.

FATHER: To that other man. Yes. And well provided for, so she would be free of me.

MOTHER: And so he'd be free of me, too.

FATHER: Yes, sir, I admit that. But great evil came of it. I meant the best. More for her than for me. *(He crosses his arms on his chest and suddenly turns to the MOTHER.)* You were never out of my sight. Not until the day he took you off to another town. How stupid. He misunderstood the pure, selfless interest I took in you. I was so happy to see the new little family that grew up around her. She can attest to that. *(Indicates the STEPDAUGHTER.)*

STEPDAUGHTER: Ah, yes. I was a wee tyke. Braids down my back. Underpants too long for my skirt. He used to wait outside the school, as I came out, to see how I was growing.

FATHER: This is shameful. Infamous.

STEPDAUGHTER: Oh? Why?

FATHER: Infamous! Infamous! *(Then suddenly to the DIRECTOR in an explanatory tone.)* Once she had left—*(Indicates the MOTHER.)* my house was suddenly empty. She'd been a burden. But she'd filled it with her presence. I was alone—like a fly with its wings torn off. And then he returned—*(Indicates the SON.)* from the country. But he wasn't my son any longer. There was no mother to link us together. He grew up on his own. All for himself. No tie of intellect. No affection to bind him to me. And then I slowly became curious about her little family I'd helped into being. It began to fill up the emptiness. I needed to know if she was happy living a simple everyday life. I wanted to know she was at peace. Away from the torments of my mind. That's when I'd watch that little girl come out of school.

STEPDAUGHTER: And indeed he did. He'd follow me. Smile. When I got home, he waved at me. Like this. I looked at him. With great wondering eyes. I didn't know him. I told my mother. She knew at once. *(The MOTHER nods.)* She didn't send me to school for a few days. Finally I went back. And there he stood—looking so ridiculous—at the school door—a paper bag in his hand. He came to me—caressed me—and brought a lovely large straw hat with a garland of May roses on it. All for me.

DIRECTOR: Excuse me. But this is all just narrative. Where's the drama?

SON: *(Contemptuously.)* Yes! Literature! Literature!

FATHER: Literature! It's not literature! It's life! It's passion!

DIRECTOR: That may be. But it's not dramatic.

FATHER: I agree. You're right. But this is only introductory. It's not to be staged. As you can see, she's *(Indicates the STEPDAUGHTER.)* no longer the little girl with braids down her back—

STEPDAUGHTER: —with her underpants showing below the skirt . . .

FATHER: *(To the DIRECTOR.)* This is where the drama begins. New. Complex.

STEPDAUGHTER: *(Coming forward, her voice gloomy, fierce.)* As soon as my father died . . .

FATHER: *(Quickly, interrupting her.)* They were thrust into poverty. They came back—I knew nothing about it—all because of her stupidity. How could she be so stupid? *(Indicates the MOTHER.)* She can't write. But the daughter or the boy could have written—that they were in need.

MOTHER: How could I have guessed he had all this feeling for us?

FATHER: Exactly. You never knew how I felt.

MOTHER: After all the years apart, and all that happened . . .

FATHER: Is it my fault he dragged you off? *(To the DIRECTOR.)* He found a job—they disappeared—overnight—it was impossible to find them. My interest in them grew less over the years. And then they returned. And then the drama broke out. Unexpectedly. Violently. And all because of the demands of my flesh . . . ! Oh, it's horrible! Horrible! Here I am— a man—alone—not old enough to do without a woman—not young enough to find one without feeling a sense of shame. Horrible! Horrible! No woman can give me love anymore. Well then, you say, do without. What a joke! To our fellow men we appear clothed in dignity—but deep inside every man knows the unconfessible things in the secret places of his heart. We give in to temptation. And immediately it's over we rise up determined to reestablish our dignity. Like a tombstone over the grave that hides any sign and memory of our shame. We're all in it together. Some of us just haven't the courage to talk about it.

STEPDAUGHTER: But they've all got the courage to do them. All of them!

FATHER: Yes. But in secret. That's why it takes courage to say them. And once you've said them, you're a cynic, and that makes you like all the others. Or maybe better. Because you're not afraid to admit to the shame of human bestiality that most men choose to deny.—And then there's woman. What kind of creature is she? She turns her gaze on you—her tantalizing, seductive gaze. You seize her—you press her to you—and she closes her eyes. The sign that says to him: "Blind yourself, for I am blind!"

STEPDAUGHTER: And when she can't close her eyes anymore? When she no longer needs to hide her shame? When she dispassionately observes the shame of men who blinded themselves without love? These intellectual complications disgust me! These philosophies that uncover the beast in man and then try to excuse him. What is more revolting, nauseating and contemptible than a man who tries to "simplify" his life with bestiality? Who throws aside every vestige of "humanity"? Purity. Chaste aspirations. Pure feelings. Idealism. Duty. Modesty. Shame. And then plunges himself into convenient remorse. Crocodile tears they call it.

DIRECTOR: Could we get to some action? So far I've heard only words.

FATHER: A fact is like a sack, sir. It won't stand up if there's nothing inside. And to make it stand, you first have to pour in all the reasons that give it being. How could I know that when they returned, poverty-stricken, she *(Indicates the MOTHER.)* would work as a dressmaker to care for her children? And especially for a woman like that . . . Madame Pace!

STEPDAUGHTER: *(To the COMPANY.)* A first-class dressmaker. In case you're interested. She works for only the cream of society. Or at least appears to. She arranges things so that fine ladies end up serving *her*. Without prejudice to other ladies, of course, who are only so-so.

MOTHER: If I had any idea that monster gave me work because she had her eye on my daughter . . .

STEPDAUGHTER: Poor Mama. *(To the DIRECTOR.)* Do you know what that woman did when I brought her my mother's finished work? She insisted that my mother had ruined the dress. It was me she made pay for it—always me—if you know what I mean. Poor mother believed she sacrificed herself for us three—*(Indicates the BOY and LITTLE GIRL.)* sitting up all night—sewing Madame Pace's dresses.

(The ACTORS show their indignation.)

DIRECTOR: *(Quickly.)* And it was there one day that you met . . . ?

STEPDAUGHTER: *(Pointing to the FATHER.)* Him! *Him!* Yes! An old client of Madame Pace's! Now there's a great scene for you! Juicy!

FATHER: When her mother arrived!

STEPDAUGHTER: *(Quickly, treacherously.) Almost* in time!

FATHER: *(Crying out.)* No! In time! In time! I recognized her! Fortunately! *In time!* And I took them back home with me. You can imagine—the two of us there—together—she—just as you see her—and I—who could no longer look her in the face.

STEPDAUGHTER: Ridiculous! After that he expected me to be modest, well-bred, a virtuous young thing—to live up to his "insane desire for moral healthiness"!

FATHER: For me drama exists in one thing—the knowledge that each of us believes himself to be a single individual. But it's not true. Each of us is many individuals, many—each of us has many possibilities of being. We are one thing for this person, and another for that, and each of them is quite different. Yet we suffer under the illusion that we are the same person for everyone. But it's not true. Not true. We perceive this—perhaps tragically—when suddenly we find ourselves caught in mid-act. And realize that not every possibility in us was involved in that act. It would be an atrocious injustice to be judged by that act alone—to be held responsible for it throughout eternity—to be pilloried—as if all of our existence had been summed up—in that one act. Do you now understand the treachery of this girl? She surprised me in a place where she should never otherwise have met me. And in an act that I should never have been doing with her. And as a result of this one fleeting, shameful moment of my life, she presumes to read the totality of my existence. And this, *this,* is what I feel most strongly about. You'll soon see the value our drama assumes from this one fact. Then, of course, there's the position of the others. His . . . *(Indicates the SON).*

SON: *(Shrugging his shoulders scornfully.)* Leave me out of this! I'm not involved!

FATHER: Not involved?

SON: I'm *not* involved! I don't *want* to be involved! I wasn't *meant* to be mixed up in this with the rest of you!

STEPDAUGHTER: Yes. We're the common, everyday, run-of-the-mill lot. He's the fine gentleman. You may have noticed. Every once in a while I throw him a contemptuous glance. He lowers his eyes. *He* knows what he's done—to me.

SON: *(Scarcely looking at her.)* I?

STEPDAUGHTER: *You! You!* It's all because of *you,* my dear, that I became a prostitute! *You! (The ACTORS are horrified.)* No! You and your attitude didn't deny us the intimacy of your home. Because we did live there. But you denied us the hospitality that makes a guest feel at ease. We were the invaders—come to disturb the kingdom of your "legitimacy"! *(To the DIRECTOR.)* I want you to see certain scenes between him and me. He claims I tyrannized them. But it was his attitude that made me take advantage of the thing that he calls "vile"! It was why I came into his house with my mother. Who is also *his* mother. And I came into his house as its mistress.

SON: *(Comes slowly forward.)* It's very easy for them, sir—to gang up against me—it's a game. But just imagine. A young son—sitting quietly at home—a knock at the door—an impudent young woman demands to see his father—for heaven knows what reason. She returns—impudent as ever—bringing with her that little girl. Finally this son sees her treating his father in an ambiguous and rude manner. She asks his father for money—but in a way that suggests that he has to give it to her—*has to*—because he's obliged to.

FATHER: I *was* obliged. Because of your mother.

SON: How am I to know that? I had never laid eyes on her. I had never heard her name mentioned. Then one day she turns up with her *(Indicates the STEPDAUGHTER.)* and the boy and the little girl. I'm told: "This is your mother, too!" And from her behavior *(Indicates the STEPDAUGH-TER.)* I gradually understand why "they" come—so suddenly. There's no way I can tell you what I feel. I don't want to. I don't even want to confess it to myself. That's why I want no part in this. I'm a dramatically "unrealized" character, sir—not at all at ease in their company. So leave me out of it.

FATHER: Excuse me! But that's exactly why you . . .

SON: *(Violently exasperated.)* How do you know what I'm like? You never raised a finger for me!

FATHER: I admit that. But it's a dramatic situation. Your aloofness—the cruelty you show to me and to your mother who returns home and sees you almost for the first time. You're grown—she doesn't recognize you—yet she knows you're her son. *(Pointing the MOTHER out to the DIRECTOR.)* Look at her. She's crying.

STEPDAUGHTER: *(Angrily, stamping her foot).* Like an idiot.

FATHER: *(Quickly, to the DIRECTOR, indicating the STEPDAUGHTER).* She can't stand him. *(Then referring again to the SON.)* He says he's not involved. Yet he's the focal point of the entire action. Look at that boy—over there—clinging to his mother—frightened. Humiliated. It's all because of him. *(Indicating the SON.)* That boy's position is the most painful of all. More than all the others. He feels like an outsider. Mortified. Humiliated. Brought into a house out of charity. *(In confidence.)* He's the image of his father—humble—hardly a word to say . . .

DIRECTOR: I suspect we'll have to cut him. Boys on stage are a real problem.

FATHER: Oh, he'll be gone before you know it. And the girl disappears, too—before he does—she goes first.

DIRECTOR: Good. Well—this is all very interesting. I suspect we may have a play here after all.

STEPDAUGHTER: *(Interrupting).* Especially with a character like me.

FATHER: *(Pushes her aside, eager to hear the DIRECTOR's decision.)* You be quiet!

DIRECTOR: *(Continues, unaware of the interruption.)* You may be on to something new here. Yes . . .

FATHER: Very new, sir.

DIRECTOR: But you did have your nerve. Coming in—throwing it at me like that . . .

FATHER: After all, sir, we were born for the stage.

DIRECTOR: Are you amateur actors?

FATHER: No. I said we were born for the stage, because . . .

DIRECTOR: Oh, come on! You're an old hand at this.

FATHER: No, sir. We just act the part we're cast in. The one we're assigned in life. But I'm a passionate man. I get excited. I become . . . theatrical. Especially when it's exalted.

DIRECTOR: Whatever. But there's no author. I suppose I could give you a name of someone who . . .

FATHER: No. No. Look. We want *you* to be the author.

DIRECTOR: Me? You must be joking!

FATHER: Yes! You! Why not?

DIRECTOR: Because I'm not an author. That's why.

FATHER: Then become one. Everyone does it these days. Nothing to it. After all, we're here, alive, in front of you.

DIRECTOR: But it's not enough.

FATHER: Why? You'll see us live out our drama.

DIRECTOR: Fine. All right. But you'll need someone to write the play.

FATHER: No. No. To take it down—maybe—as we act it—scene by scene. But for now just a sketch is good enough. Then we'll rehearse.

DIRECTOR: *(Coming back onto the stage.)* Hm. I'm almost tempted. Could be fun. At least we could try . . .

FATHER: Wait till you see our scenes. I can tell you what they are right now.

DIRECTOR: Yes. I'm tempted. Really tempted. Let's give it a try. Come into my office. *(To the ACTORS.)* Take a break. Don't go far. Be back in fifteen or twenty minutes. *(To the FATHER.)* Let's see what we can come up with. It could be extraordinary . . .

FATHER: No doubt about it. But shouldn't they *(Indicates the OTHER CHARACTERS.)* come along, too?

DIRECTOR: Of course. Come on. Come on. *(Starts off and turns to the ACTORS.)* Fifteen minutes! Don't forget!

(The DIRECTOR and the SIX CHARACTERS cross the stage and go off. The ACTORS look at one another in astonishment.)

MALE LEAD: Is he serious? What the hell's he trying to do?

YOUNG ACTOR: This is ridiculous.

A THIRD ACTOR: He expects us to improvise a play?

YOUNG ACTOR: Why not? Like the old Commedia dell' arte.

FEMALE LEAD: Well, count me out.

INGENUE: Me, too.

A FOURTH ACTOR: Who the hell do they think they are! *(Alluding to the CHARACTERS.)*

THIRD ACTOR: They're nuts, if you ask me. Or crooks. One or the other.

YOUNG ACTOR: Does he really take them seriously?

MALE LEAD: This is crazy.

A FIFTH ACTOR: I'm kind of enjoying it.

THIRD ACTOR: Oh, what the hell, let's give it a chance!

(And in conversation the ACTORS leave the stage; some go out the rear door, others return to their dressing rooms. The curtain remains up. The performance is interrupted for twenty minutes.)

END OF ACT I

ACT TWO

The bell rings to warn the audience that the performance is about to resume. The ACTORS, the STAGE MANAGER, the CREW HEAD, the PROMPTER, and the PROPERTY MAN assemble on stage from the dressing rooms, through the rear door, and some even through the auditorium. At the same time, the DIRECTOR and the SIX CHARACTERS come on stage from his office. The house lights are lowered and the former stage lighting is resumed.

DIRECTOR: Are we all here? Let's go. Let's go. Your attention, please? I think we can begin. Is the crew head here?

CREW HEAD: Right here, sir.

DIRECTOR: I'll need a parlor scene. Two wings. A drop with a door. Please hurry.

(The CREW HEAD runs off and goes about setting up the scene while the DIRECTOR makes arrangements with the STAGE MANAGER, the PROPERTY MAN, the PROMPTER, and the ACTORS. The set that has been brought out is painted in pink and gold stripes.)

DIRECTOR: *(To the PROPERTY MAN.)* See if you can dig up a sofa or divan in the prop room.

PROPERTY MAN: How about a green one?

STEPDAUGHTER: No. No. Green won't do. It was yellow. Flowers. Plush. Very comfortable.

PROPERTY MAN: I'm afraid not. Sorry.

DIRECTOR: Doesn't matter. Give me what you've got.

STEPDAUGHTER: Doesn't matter? Madame Pace's famous sofa?

DIRECTOR: Please. This is a rehearsal. And don't interrupt. *(To the STAGE MANAGER.)* See if there's a long, low shop window.

STEPDAUGHTER: And a table—a small table—mahogany—for the light blue envelope.

STAGE MANAGER: *(To the DIRECTOR.)* There's a little gold-painted number . . .

DIRECTOR: Good. Let's have it.

FATHER: And the large mirror.

STEPDAUGHTER: And the screen. I can't possibly do without a screen.

STAGE MANAGER: Yes, ma'am. Don't worry. We've got a whole room full of those . . .

DIRECTOR: *(To the STEPDAUGHTER.)* And . . . clothes stands. Right?

STEPDAUGHTER: Lots of them.

DIRECTOR: *(To the STAGE MANAGER.)* Bring up all you've got.

STAGE MANAGER: Right away, sir. I'll get right on it.

(The STAGE MANAGER goes off to take care of matters. While the DIREC-TOR is talking to the PROMPTER and then to the SIX CHARACTERS and the ACTORS, the STAGE MANAGER has STAGEHANDS bring on the furniture and props and arranges them as he thinks suitable.)

DIRECTOR: *(To the PROMPTER.)* Now. Take your seat and I'll give you the outline act by act. *(Hands him several sheets of paper.)* But now I have to make a rather strange request. I hope you don't mind.

PROMPTER: You want me to take it down in shorthand.

DIRECTOR: *(Pleasantly surprised.)* Wonderful! Do you know how?

PROMPTER: I may not be the world's greatest ASM, but wait till you see my shorthand!

DIRECTOR: You're a prince. *(To a STAGEHAND.)* Get paper out of my office—all you can find.

(The STAGEHAND goes off and soon returns with a large amount of paper that he hands to the PROMPTER.)

DIRECTOR: *(To the PROMPTER.)* Follow the scene we're doing. Be careful. Try to get down the main points. *(To the ACTORS.)* Clear the stage, please. No. No. Over here. *(Waves them over to the left.)* And pay very close attention.

FEMALE LEAD: Excuse me, sir. Will we . . .

DIRECTOR: *(Forestalling her fears.)* Never fear, my dear. You won't have to improvise.

MALE LEAD: Then what will we be doing?

DIRECTOR: Nothing. For the moment you sit and watch. Rôles will be assigned later. This is just a first attempt. As far as it goes. And they'll be doing it. *(Indicating the SIX CHARACTERS.)*

FATHER: *(As if he had fallen from the clouds into the midst of the confusion on stage.)* We'll be doing what? What do you mean?

DIRECTOR: We're giving it a try. A rehearsal for their benefit. *(Indicating the ACTORS.)*

FATHER: But if we're the characters . . .

DIRECTOR: Very well. "Characters," if you prefer! But it's not the "characters" who do the acting. It's the actors. The characters live in the script. *(Pointing to the PROMPTER.)* Once we *have* a script, that is.

FATHER: Exactly. But there *is* no script. And they have the characters alive in front of them.

DIRECTOR: Ah! Great! Are you planning on doing it all yourselves? Act? In front of an audience?

FATHER: Yes. Just as we are.

DIRECTOR: Good God! What a show that would be!

MALE LEAD: In which case, why are we here?

DIRECTOR: Surely you don't imagine that you can act? What a ludicrous proposition! *(The ACTORS burst into laughter.)* You see? They're laughing. *(Remembering something.)* Come to think of it, I might as well do the casting right now. It almost casts itself. *(To the SECOND FEMALE LEAD.)* You play the Mother. *(To the FATHER.)* We'll have to find a name for her.

FATHER: Amalia.

DIRECTOR: That's your wife's name. We don't want to call her by her real name, for God's sake!

FATHER: Why? It's her name. But if that's the woman to play her . . . *(Indicates the SECOND FEMALE LEAD with a slight gesture.)* I see *that* woman *(Indicates the MOTHER.)* as Amalia, sir. But do as you like. *(He becomes more confused.)* I don't know what to say anymore. My own words sound false to me. They have the wrong tone . . .

DIRECTOR: We'll find it. Don't worry. And if "Amalia" you want, then "Amalia" you get. Whatever. Let's see now. *(To the JUVENILE LEAD.)* You play the Son. *(To the FEMALE LEAD.)* You, of course, play the Stepdaughter.

STEPDAUGHTER: *(Excitedly.)* What? Me? That woman there? *(Bursts out laughing.)*

DIRECTOR: *(Angrily.)* May I ask what's so funny!

FEMALE LEAD: *(Indignant.)* Don't laugh at me! You could at least have a little respect!

STEPDAUGHTER: I'm sorry. I wasn't laughing at you.

DIRECTOR: *(To the STEPDAUGHTER.)* You should feel honored to be played by . . .

FEMALE LEAD: *(Sarcastically.)* . . . "that woman there"!

STEPDAUGHTER: Please. I didn't mean you. Believe me. I was laughing at myself. I can't see myself in you. I mean . . . we're not alike . . .

FATHER: Yes, exactly. Look, sir. Everything we feel . . .

DIRECTOR: Everything you feel! Whatever *that* is, I suppose you think you've got a monopoly on it. Forget it!

FATHER: Aren't even our feelings our own?

DIRECTOR: No. They're material for the actors. They flesh it out. Give it form, voice, gesture. And I assure you, my actors have "felt" better material than this. Your little drama isn't exactly top-drawer. If it works, you'll have them to thank for it.

FATHER: I know. But for us, who are as we are, as we stand here before you, with these bodies, these features . . . we suffer horribly when . . .

DIRECTOR: *(Interrupting impatiently.)* But, good God, man, they'll have makeup.

FATHER: Yes. But the gestures. The voices . . .

DIRECTOR: All right! All right, now! Just one minute! Number one: You will not be acting yourselves. Number two: We have actors to act you. And number three: That's that!

FATHER: I understand. I also begin to see why our creator didn't want to put us on stage. I mean no offense. But how can someone I don't even know . . . play me?

MALE LEAD: *(Rises and comes over to him with some dignity, followed by the a group of YOUNG ACTRESSES who are laughing.)* Which would be me, sir—if you have no objection.

FATHER: *(Humbly, mellifluously.)* I am deeply honored. *(Bows.)* But however much this gentleman tries with his art to absorb me into himself . . . *(Becoming confused.)*

MALE LEAD: Go on. Go on.

(The ACTRESSES laugh.)

FATHER: I mean, if he acts me . . . even with the help of makeup . . . and with his figure . . . *(The ACTORS laugh.)* acting me as I really am will be difficult. But his looks don't matter. What matters is how he interprets me—how he sees me—if he sees me at all. Which could be different from how I see myself. All of this must be considered by anyone who comes to judge us.

DIRECTOR: He's already worried about the critics! Let's let the critics write what they want, shall we? Let's first worry about getting the play on its feet—assuming that ever happens. *(Takes a few steps and surveys the stage.)* Are we ready? Is the stage set up? *(To the ACTORS and to the SIX CHARACTERS.)* Don't clutter the stage. Let me see what it looks like. *(Steps down into the auditorium.)* We can't waste anymore time. *(To the STEPDAUGHTER.)* How does the set look?

STEPDAUGHTER: I don't recognize it.

DIRECTOR: What did you expect? Madame Pace's backroom? *(To the FATHER.)* You said a room with flowered wallpaper?

FATHER: Yes. White.

DIRECTOR: White it's not. And it has stripes. So much for that. What about the furniture? Bring that small table a little farther downstage. *(The STAGEHANDS do as directed.)*

DIRECTOR *(To the PROPERTY MAN.)* We'll need an envelope. Light blue. Give it to that gentleman. *(Indicates the FATHER.)*

PROPERTY MAN: For a letter?

DIRECTOR and FATHER: Yes. For a letter.

PROPERTY MAN: Right away, sir. *(Goes off.)*

DIRECTOR: All right. Let's get started. Scene one. The young lady. *(The FEMALE LEAD comes downstage.)* No. No. Please. Not yet. I meant the girl. *(Indicates the STEPDAUGHTER.)* You just watch—

STEPDAUGHTER: *(Adding quickly.)* —how I live it.

FEMALE LEAD: *(Resentfully.)* Don't worry, dearie, once I'm into it, I'll be "living it" just fine.

DIRECTOR: *(Hands at his head.)* Please! Let's not have any bickering! All right? Now! Scene one. The young lady with Madame Pace. Oh, my God! *(Looks around confused, then comes back on stage.)* Where's our Madame Pace?

FATHER: She's not with us, sir.

DIRECTOR: So what do we do?

FATHER: But she's alive. Alive as we are.

DIRECTOR: Fine. But where is she?

FATHER: I'll take care of it. *(Turns to the ACTRESSES.)* Ladies. Please. Lend me your hats. For a moment. Please.

ACTRESSES: *(A bit surprised, laughing, in chorus.)* What?—Our hats?— What's he talking about?—Why?—Oh, really!

DIRECTOR: What are you doing with the hats? *(The ACTORS laugh.)*

FATHER: Nothing. I want to put them on these clothes stands. Could I have a coat, too? Ladies? Please?

THE ACTORS: Coats? Jeez! The guy's a lunatic!

ACTRESSES. But why?—Only the coat?

FATHER: To hang them. Here. For a moment. Please? A favor? *(The ACTRESSES remove their hats, and one or two of them a coat, laughing as they do so, then go over to the set and hang them here and there on the clothes stands.)*

ACTRESSES. Oh, why not.—There you are.—This is really crazy.—Do we have to put them on display?

FATHER: Exactly. Just like that.

DIRECTOR: May I ask why?

FATHER: Well, you see, sir—if we really set the stage properly . . . make it look as real as possible . . . who knows? Maybe Madame Pace will be attracted by the articles of her trade and come herself . . . *(He invites them to look at the door at the back of the stage.)* Look! Look there!

(The door in the rear opens and MADAME PACE enters and takes a few steps forward. She is an enormous, fat old hag, wearing a horrible carrot-colored wig with a flaming rose stuck into one side, in the Spanish manner, heavily made up, and dressed with clumsy elegance in a red silk dress. In one hand she carries an ostrich feather fan, in the other, raised hand, she holds a lighted cigarette. Immediately upon seeing this apparition, the ACTORS and DIRECTOR make a headlong rush down the steps leading into the auditorium with a cry of horror as if they intended to dash up the aisles. The STEPDAUGHTER, however, runs over to MADAME PACE as if greeting her old mistress.)

STEPDAUGHTER: There! There she is!

FATHER: *(Radiant.)* It's her! I told you! There she is!

DIRECTOR *(Recovered from the initial surprise, indignant.)* What the hell kind of a trick is that!

(The next four speeches are spoken almost simultaneously.)

MALE LEAD: What's going on!

YOUNG ACTOR: How did she get here?

INGENUE: They've been holding her in reserve!

FEMALE LEAD: Vulgar tricks, if you ask me!

FATHER: *(Rising above the protests.)* Excuse me! Please! Excuse me! Why are you trying to destroy this prodigy of reality in the name of a vulgar, commonplace sense of truth? This reality that has been evoked by the magic of the stage? It has more right to be here than you. It is much truer than you. Which of you will play Madame Pace? But here *is* Madame Pace. Herself. The actress who plays her will be much less true. Because here is Madame Pace. In person. As you saw. My daughter recognized her at once. Watch the scene now. Watch it.

(Hesitantly the DIRECTOR and the ACTORS return to the stage. The scene between the STEPDAUGHTER and MADAME PACE began so quietly and naturally during the ACTORS' protestations and the FATHER's reply that it would not communicate on a stage. At the FATHER's insistence that the ACTORS watch the scene, they see that MADAME PACE has put her hand under the STEPDAUGHTER's chin to raise her head and is talking

to her. Her speech, however, is unintelligible and the ACTORS' attention begins to wane.)

DIRECTOR: Well?

MALE LEAD: What's she saying?

FEMALE LEAD: I can't understand a word.

INGENUE: Louder! Louder!

STEPDAUGHTER: *(Leaves MADAME PACE, who has an indefinable smile on her face, and approaches the ACTORS.)* Louder? What do you mean, louder? You don't say such things out loud. I did it only to shame him. *(Pointing to the FATHER.)* It was my revenge. But with Madame Pace it's quite another matter. It could mean prison for her.

DIRECTOR: Really? Well! So that's how it is. But, my dear, this is the theater, you must be heard. We're on stage here with you and can't hear a thing. What about an audience? In the auditorium? The scene's got to communicate. Speak up. You're among yourselves. We're not even here. Not listening. Pretend you're alone—together—in a room at the rear of Madame Pace's shop—with no one to hear you. *(The STEPDAUGH-TER, a somewhat malicious smile on her face, elegantly and charmingly wags her finger two or three times in disagreement.)* What do you mean, no?

STEPDAUGHTER: *(Quietly, in a mysterious voice.)* There *is* someone who'll hear us if she *(Indicates MADAME PACE.)* speaks up.

DIRECTOR: *(In consternation.)* Someone else you've had in hiding?!
(The ACTORS are on the verge of again plunging from the stage.)

FATHER: No, sir! No, no, no! She means me. I'm behind that door. Waiting. Madame Pace knows that. I'll get in place. So I can make my entrance when . . . *(He is on the verge of going.)*

DIRECTOR: *(Holding him back.)* No. I'm sorry. Wait. This is a theater. You must honor its conventions. Before you come on . . .

STEPDAUGHTER: *(Interrupts him.)* No. Now. Now. I'm dying to play the scene, dying. If he's ready, so am I.

DIRECTOR: *(Shouting.)* But first finish the scene between you and her. *(Indicates MADAME PACE.)* Do you understand?

STEPDAUGHTER: But you already know what she's telling me. My mother's work was done badly again. The dress is ruined. And if she's to continue helping us in our misfortune, I must be patient.

MADAME PACE: *(Advances with a grand air of importance.)* But, yes, señor. I no want to be hard. I no want to take advantage . . .

DIRECTOR: *(Shocked.)* What? What is she . . . ? Does she talk like that? *(The ACTORS burst out laughing.)*

STEPDAUGHTER: *(Also laughing.)* Yes. I'm afraid so. Half English, half Spanish. It's very funny.

MADAME PACE: Is no nice of you, señor. You laugh. I push myself to hablar your English. Is no easy.

DIRECTOR: No. No. It's very wrong of us. You just continue, Madame. It's wonderful. Anything to lighten up the crudity of this situation. Thank God! A little comedy! You go on talking. Just like that. It's wonderful.

STEPDAUGHTER: Wonderful? Why not? Propositioning someone in language like that is bound to get a laugh. Sounds like a joke. Imagine hearing that a "viechio señor" wants to "amusarse con migo!" Right, Madame?

MADAME PACE: No. No so old. Only no so young. Si? And if he no please you . . . at least he have prudencia.

(The ACTORS, absorbed in the scene, have been virtually unaware of the MOTHER, who now, to the ACTORS' amazement and consternation, storms over to MADAME PACE, rips off her wig, and throws it to the ground. The ACTORS, amused, try to restrain her.)

MOTHER: Witch! Witch! Murderer! My poor daughter!

STEPDAUGHTER: *(Rushes over to calm her MOTHER.)* No! No! Mother, no! Please! Calm down!

FATHER: *(Rushing over at the same time.)* Calm down! Don't get excited! Come, sit down.

MOTHER: Then first get that woman out of my sight!

(The DIRECTOR has also rushed over to the encounter.)

STEPDAUGHTER: *(To the DIRECTOR.)* I'm sorry. My mother can't stay here.

FATHER: *(To the DIRECTOR.)* The two of them can't be here together. That's why Madame Pace wasn't with us at first. If they're here together, they'll give it all away.

DIRECTOR: So what? It's a rehearsal. The first one. I need to see everything. I'll make sense of it later. Right now I just need the main points of the action. *(He leads the MOTHER back to her seat.)* Come. Come now. Let's sit back down.

(The STEPDAUGHTER has meanwhile returned to the scene and turns to MADAME PACE.)

STEPDAUGHTER: Continue, Madame.

MADAME PACE: *(Offended.)* No! No! Thank you very much! I no do nada with your madre present.

STEPDAUGHTER: Come on. Let the "viechio señor" in. So he can "amusarse con migo!" *(To the others, imperiously.)* We have no choice but to play this scene. Let's start. *(To MADAME PACE.)* You can go.

MADAME PACE: Ah, yes . . . I go, I go . . . seguramente. *(She exits furiously, picking up her wig and putting it on her head with a scornful look at the ACTORS, who applaud her mockingly.)*

STEPDAUGHTER: *(To the FATHER.)* Make your entrance now. Don't worry about entering again. Come over here. Act as if you'd just come in. All right. I'm standing here. Modestly. My eyes lowered.—Well, let's hear it. Let's hear that special voice of yours. That special tone. Say "Good afternoon, miss!"

DIRECTOR: *(Who by now has returned to the auditorium.)* Excuse me. Who's the director? You or I? *(To the FATHER, who looks perplexed and undecided.)* All right. Go on. Do what she says. Go all the way upstage. Don't go off. And come forward again.

(The FATHER, troubled and pale, does as he is told. But he is already absorbed in the reality of his created life. He comes forward, smiling, as if oblivious of the drama that lies ahead of him. The ACTORS watch the beginning scene intently.)

DIRECTOR: *(Whispers quickly to the PROMPTER.)* Ready? Pay attention. Get down as much as you can.

THE SCENE

FATHER: *(Coming forward and speaking in a different tone of voice).* Good afternoon, miss!

STEPDAUGHTER: *(Her head bowed with restrained disgust).* Good afternoon!

FATHER: *(Studies her a bit, then looks under the hat that almost hides her face and notices that she is still rather young; he exclaims almost to himself, a bit out of complacency, but also from fear of compromising himself in a risky adventure.)* Oh. I see. Hm. This isn't your first time here? Is it?

STEPDAUGHTER: *(As above.)* No, sir.

FATHER: Then you've been here before? *(Since she nods affirmatively.)* More than once? *(Waits a moment for her reply, then looks again under the brim of the hat, smiles, and says:)* Well, then . . . Then there's no need to be so . . . May I take your hat?

STEPDAUGHTER: *(No longer able to withhold her disgust, quickly, to forestall him.)* No. I'll take it off myself. *(Trembling nervously, she quickly takes it off.)*

(The MOTHER, together with the SON and the two small CHILDREN who cling to her, sits watching the scene on the side opposite the ACTORS. She is in torment, and follows the progress of the scene between the FATHER and the STEPDAUGHTER with expressions that vacillate between sorrow, indignation, anxiety, and horror. From time to time she hides her face and sobs.)

MOTHER: Oh, God! My God!

FATHER: *(Stops as if turned to stone by the sob, then continues in his earlier tone of voice.)* Give it here. I'll hang it up. *(He takes the hat from her hand.)* Such a sweet, charming little head. It deserves a much smarter hat than this. Let me choose one . . . from Madame's collection. May I?

INGENUE: *(Interrupting.)* Those are our hats!

DIRECTOR: *(Quickly, furious.)* For God's sake, shut up! This is no time for jokes. We're rehearsing—in case you haven't noticed. *(To the STEP-DAUGHTER.)* Take it from where you left off.

STEPDAUGHTER: *(Continuing.)* Thank you, sir. No.

FATHER: Please—don't say no. You have to—I'll be upset. Look at them. Aren't they lovely? And it would please Madame—that's why she has them here.

STEPDAUGHTER: No. No. I couldn't wear it.

FATHER: Because of home? They'd wonder where you got it? I'll tell you what to do—what to say—when you get home.

STEPDAUGHTER: *(Almost unable to control herself.)* No. It's not that. Well . . . you can see . . . I'm in mourning.

FATHER: In mourning. Yes. I'm sorry. I see now . . . excuse me. I'm terribly ashamed . . .

STEPDAUGHTER: *(Pulls herself together and tries to suppress her indignation and nausea.)* No—please—I should thank you. Don't be sorry. Don't be ashamed. Just forget it—forget what I said. I should do the same. *(Forcing herself to laugh and continuing.)* I should forget I'm dressed like this . . .

DIRECTOR: *(Interrupts, climbs back on stage and talks to the PROMPTER.)* Stop! Hold on! Don't take down that last bit . . . *(To the FATHER and the STEPDAUGHTER.)* Very good! Marvelous! *(To the FATHER alone.)* You can go on now—as arranged. *(To the ACTORS.)* That scene with the hat? Lovely, don't you think?

STEPDAUGHTER: But the best is still to come. Why have we stopped?

DIRECTOR: Patience. Please. *(To the ACTORS.)* Just play it a little lighter.

MALE LEAD: It could use a little polish.

FEMALE LEAD: Nothing to it. *(To the MALE LEAD:)* Shall we?

MALE LEAD: Why not? I'll get in place . . . *(Goes to the upstage door to make his entrance.)*

DIRECTOR: *(To the FEMALE LEAD.)* All right. The scene between you and Madame Pace is over. I'll write it down afterwards. You stand here . . . Where are you going?

FEMALE LEAD: Hold on. I want to put on my hat. *(Removes her hat from the clothes stand.)*

DIRECTOR: Good. Now just stand there. Bow your head a little.

STEPDAUGHTER: *(Amused.)* But she's not dressed in black.

FEMALE LEAD: Oh, but I will be, dear. And much more effectively.

DIRECTOR: *(To the STEPDAUGHTER.)* Quiet, please! Just watch. You might learn something. *(He claps his hands.)* Let's go! Let's go! Your entrance . . . *(The DIRECTOR returns to the auditorium to see the scene from out front.)*

(The upstage door opens and the MALE LEAD comes forward with the lively and informal manner of an old gallant. The playing of this scene by the ACTORS should from the start be quite different from what it was before. At the same time it must never, even to the slightest degree, have the feel of parody about it, but rather of having been touched up. Naturally the STEPDAUGHTER and the FATHER fail to recognize themselves in the FEMALE LEAD and the MALE LEAD, even though they are speaking the same words. They express their surprise, suffering, and wonderment in various ways, with smiles, gestures, and open protests. The voice of the PROMPTER is heard clearly throughout as he prompts them in their lines.)

MALE LEAD: "Good afternoon, miss!"

FATHER: *(Immediately, unable to restrain himself.)* No—no!

(Noticing the way the MALE LEAD enters, the STEPDAUGHTER bursts into laughter.)

DIRECTOR: *(In a rage).* Shut up! Stop laughing! We'll never get anywhere this way!

STEPDAUGHTER: *(Moves away from the proscenium.)* I'm sorry. I couldn't help it. *(Indicating the FEMALE LEAD.)* The lady's just standing there. But if she's supposed to be me, and somebody said "Good afternoon" to me like that, and in that tone of voice . . . I'd burst out laughing. And that's what I did.

FATHER: *(Also comes forward a bit.)* Yes—that's it—his manner—his tone . . .

DIRECTOR: What manner? What tone? Sit down? Please? So we can rehearse?

MALE LEAD: *(Comes forward.)* Look—if I'm supposed to play an old man coming into a house of somewhat dubious reputation . . .

DIRECTOR: Just ignore him! Please! Take it from the top! It was great! *(Waiting for the MALE LEAD to begin.)* Well?

MALE LEAD: "Good afternoon, miss!"

FEMALE LEAD: "Good afternoon!"

MALE LEAD: *(Imitating the FATHER's action, first looking up at her face from under the brim of her hat, then expressing very clearly his satisfaction and then his secret fear.)* "Oh. I see. Hm. This isn't your first time here? I hope . . ."

FATHER *(Correcting him).* Not "I hope." I said: "Is it?" ". . . not your first time here? Is it?"!!

DIRECTOR: You say "Is it?" It's a question.

MALE LEAD: *(Indicating the PROMPTER.)* He said "I hope."

DIRECTOR: "I hope"! "Is it?" Who cares! It doesn't matter! Just keep it going. And don't make it a caricature. Here—let me show you . . . *(Climbs on stage and repeats the scene.)* "Good afternoon, miss!"

FEMALE LEAD: "Good afternoon!"

DIRECTOR: "Oh. I see. Hm." *(He turns to the MALE LEAD to show him how to look under the brim of the FEMALE LEAD's hat.)* Surprise. Fear. Satisfaction. *(Then turning back to the FEMALE LEAD.)* "This isn't your first time here? Is it?" *(To the MALE LEAD again.)* You see? *(Turning back to the FEMALE LEAD.)* And now you. "No, sir." *(Back to the MALE LEAD.)* So . . . make it a little more . . . free. Let it flow. *(Goes back down into the auditorium.)*

FEMALE LEAD: "No, sir."

MALE LEAD: "Then you've been here before? More than once?"

DIRECTOR: No! No! Stop! First let her nod. "Then you've been here before?"
(The FEMALE LEAD raises her head slightly, half-closes her eyes to signify disgust, and when the DIRECTOR says "Now," she inclines her head twice.)

STEPDAUGHTER: *(No longer able to contain herself.)* Oh, God! *(She quickly presses her hand to her mouth to keep from laughing.)*

DIRECTOR: *(Turning around).* What is it?

STEPDAUGHTER: *(Quickly).* No. Nothing.

DIRECTOR: *(To the MALE LEAD).* You're on.

MALE LEAD: "More than once? Well, then! Then there's no need to be so . . . May I take your hat?"

(The MALE LEAD has said this speech in such a tone of voice and with such gestures that the STEPDAUGHTER, whose hand has been pressed to her mouth, can no longer keep from laughing.)

FEMALE LEAD: *(Exasperated, returns to her seat.)* I don't need to be made a fool of by that woman!

MALE LEAD: Me, too! I've had it!

DIRECTOR: *(Yelling at the STEPDAUGHTER.)* Stop that! I won't have anymore!

STEPDAUGHTER: Yes. I'm sorry. I . . . I'm sorry!

DIRECTOR: Don't you have any manners? What an arrogant . . . !

FATHER: Yes, sir! You're right! Excuse us . . .

DIRECTOR: *(Goes back on stage.)* Excuse? Why? It's disgusting!

FATHER: Yes, sir. But it *is* rather strange.

DIRECTOR: Strange? What's strange?

FATHER: I admire your actors, sir. This gentleman . . . *(Indicates the MALE LEAD.)* the lady . . . *(Indicates the FEMALE LEAD.)* But in reality . . . they're not *us!*

DIRECTOR: I should hope not! They're *actors!* How can they be *you?*

FATHER: Yes—that's right—actors. They act our parts very well—both of them—but the effect . . . it's so different. They should *be* us, but they're *not.*

DIRECTOR: Then what are they?

FATHER: They're . . . they're themselves. Not us . . .

DIRECTOR: Exactly—as it should be. I've told you that.

FATHER: Yes. I understand, I understand.

DIRECTOR: Then let's have an end. *(To the ACTORS.)* We'll rehearse afterwards—by ourselves—as usual. I can't stand authors. Nothing ever pleases them. *(To the FATHER and the STEPDAUGHTER.)* All right. Let's take it again. And try not to laugh—make an effort.

STEPDAUGHTER: Don't worry. I promise. There's a nice little bit coming up for me.

DIRECTOR: So. After you say: "Don't be sorry. Don't be ashamed. Just forget it. Forget what I said. I should do the same," you *(Addressing the FATHER.)* should answer immediately: "I understand. Yes. I understand." And then you ask her . . .

STEPDAUGHTER: *(Interrupting.)* What?

DIRECTOR: Why she's in mourning.

STEPDAUGHTER: No, sir! No! When I told him that it was useless for me to think about being in mourning, do you know what he said? "Good. Then let's just take the dress off."

DIRECTOR: Oh! Wonderful! That'll bring the house down!

STEPDAUGHTER: But it's the truth.

DIRECTOR: So what? This is the theater. Truth goes only so far.

STEPDAUGHTER: Then what do you want?

DIRECTOR: You'll see. Just leave it to me.

STEPDAUGHTER: No—no . . . you're trying to paste up some sentimental little scene out of my disgust. Out of all the cruel and vile reasons I am what I am. When he asks me why I'm in mourning, I have to answer with tears in my eyes that my papa died two months ago. He has to say *exactly* what he said. "Good. Then let's just take the dress off." And I . . . with two months' mourning in my heart . . . went behind that screen . . . and with these fingers trembling with shame and disgust . . . unbuttoned my blouse . . . took off my skirt . . .

DIRECTOR: *(Running his hands through his hair.)* Good God! What are you saying!

STEPDAUGHTER: *(Screaming as if insane.)* The truth! The truth!

DIRECTOR: I believe you! I believe it's the truth! I don't deny it! And I understand your horror! But you must understand. You can't put this kind of thing on stage. It's impossible.

STEPDAUGHTER: Impossible? All right! Thank you! I'm through!

DIRECTOR: No. Please. Be reasonable.

STEPDAUGHTER: Thank you—no—I'm through! It's obvious. In your office you "arranged" what was possible on stage. Thank you! I understand! *He* wants to get to his famous *(Ironically.)* "spiritual conflict" without delay! But I want to act *my* drama, too! *My* drama!

DIRECTOR: *(Shoulders shaking with annoyance.)* Ah! Finally! There we have it! *Your* drama! But it's not simply *your* drama! It's *everyone's* drama! *(Indicating the FATHER.)* Your *father's!* Your *mother's!* You can't just dominate the stage to the exclusion of everyone else! It's a unit! It's harmonious! Every part has its place! The aim is to pack them all inside a single frame, and then act what is actable! I'm well aware that each one carries a complete life inside him and wants to present it to the world. But you can't do that. On stage you can present only what's necessary. You take *all* the characters into consideration. And you have to hint at the unrevealed life in each of them. It would be handy if each had his own monologue or could give a public lecture on what boils and seethes inside him. *(Good humored and conciliatory.)* You have to hold yourself back—for your own sake. This fury and exasperation and disgust of yours could work against you. You must admit that you've confessed to having had many men before him in Madame Pace's shop. And more than once.

STEPDAUGHTER: *(Bows her head, then, after a pause, in a more profound tone of voice.)* True. But those others were no one but *him.*

DIRECTOR: *(Uncomprehending.)* I'm sorry. I don't understand.

STEPDAUGHTER: When a person goes wrong, the one responsible for the first fault is responsible for all the others. For me, it's *him.* From before I was born. Look at him. It's written all over him.

DIRECTOR: Fine—but look at the remorse—weighing him down. Doesn't that count for anything? Give him a chance. Let him act it out.

STEPDAUGHTER: But how? How *can* he act out all his "noble remorse"? All his "moral torments"? You're trying to spare him the horror of one day finding in his arms that child. Barely a woman. And already a whore. Whose dress he asked to be removed. That child he once waited for outside the school door. *(Her last words are spoken in a tremulous voice.)*
(The MOTHER, hearing these words, is overcome by an unspeakable sorrow that at first she expresses in repressed sobs. Finally she breaks out in a fit of unrestrained crying. All are deeply moved. There is a long pause.)

STEPDAUGHTER: *(Gravely and resolutely, after the MOTHER has become quieter.)* We're here today without an audience. Tomorrow you'll put on our play—as you see fit—in any way you like. But don't you first want to see our drama? As it *really* existed? See it *flash* to life, in front of you?

DIRECTOR: There's nothing I'd like better. I need to see as much as possible. To know what to use . . .

STEPDAUGHTER: All right. Then send the mother away.

MOTHER: *(Raising her soft weeping to a sharp cry.)* No—no—don't let them do it, sir! Don't let them do it!

DIRECTOR: *(To the MOTHER.)* Just to watch, dear lady—just to watch.

MOTHER: I can't bear it! I can't!

DIRECTOR: But it's already happened. I don't understand.

MOTHER: No! It's happening *now!* It happens all the *time!* My torment isn't pretended! I *live*, I *breath* every *minute* of my torment! It never ends! These two children. Have you heard them speak? They can't speak anymore. They cling to me only to keep my torment alive, and present. They don't exist anymore. And she . . . *(Indicating the STEPDAUGHTER.)* she ran away. She's lost. And if she's here—here in front of my eyes—it's only to renew the torment I suffered for her.

FATHER: *(Solemnly.)* The eternal moment. Just as I said, sir. *(Indicating the STEPDAUGHTER.)* She's here to pin me for all eternity to that one fleeting and shameful moment of my life. She has no choice. She can't leave it. And you, sir, can't spare me my agony either.

DIRECTOR: I never said I didn't want to present it. It's the core of the first act. Up to where she surprises you. *(Indicates the MOTHER.)*

FATHER: That's right. Because it's my sentence. All of our suffering culminates there. In her final cry. *(Indicates the MOTHER.)*

STEPDAUGHTER: I still hear it. It drove me mad. You can play me any way you want. It doesn't matter. Even dressed. If only my arms are bare. Only my arms. Because standing like this—*(Goes to the FATHER and lays her head against his chest)* my head against his chest—my arms around his neck . . . I could see a vein . . . throbbing . . . in my arm . . . here. And as if disgusted by that throbbing vein, I closed my eyes, horrified, and buried my head in his chest. *(Turning to the MOTHER.)* Scream, Mama! Scream! *(She buries her head in the FATHER's chest, raises her shoulders as if to block out the scream, and adds in a voice of intense emotion.)* Scream as you screamed then!

MOTHER: *(Rushes over to separate the two of them.)* No! My daughter! My daughter! *(And after having torn her daughter away.)* Brute! Brute! She's my daughter! Can't you see! She's my daughter!

DIRECTOR: *(At the scream he retreats to the edge of the stage amid excitement among the ACTORS.)* That's it! That's it! And then curtain! Curtain!

FATHER: *(Rushes over to him, convulsively.)* That's how it was! That's how it happened!

DIRECTOR: *(Convinced, admiration in his voice.)* Perfect curtain line! Perfect! Curtain! Curtain!

(At the DIRECTOR's repeated cries, the STAGEHAND on the curtain lets the curtain fall, leaving the DIRECTOR and the FATHER alone in front of it.)

DIRECTOR: *(Looking up, his arms raised.)* What an idiot! I say "curtain" and he brings down the curtain! I meant that's where the act ends! *(To the FATHER as he parts the curtain to get back onstage.)* Wonderful! Wonderful! It's a great act ending! Great! It's a great first act, too!

(When the curtain rises we see that the previous set has been struck and that the STAGEHANDS have set up a small garden fountain. The ACTORS are seated in a row on one side of the stage, and on the other side are the Characters. The DIRECTOR is standing in a meditative attitude in the middle of the stage, his hand over his mouth.)

DIRECTOR: *(Shrugging his shoulders after a brief pause.)* All right! Second act! Just leave it to me. As arranged. Everything'll turn out fine.

STEPDAUGHTER: Our entry into his house. *(Indicates the FATHER.)* In spite of him. *(Indicates the SON.)*

DIRECTOR: *(Impatiently.)* All right! Leave it to me!

STEPDAUGHTER: Just so it's clear. That it was against his wishes. In spite of him.

MOTHER: *(From the corner, shaking her head.)* For all the good that's come of it . . .

STEPDAUGHTER: *(Quickly, to her.)* It doesn't matter. The more done against us, the greater his remorse.

DIRECTOR: *(Impatiently.)* Yes! I understand! I'll take it into account! Just don't get excited.

MOTHER: *(Supplicating.)* I beg you, sir. Make it clear. I did all I could to . . .

STEPDAUGHTER: *(Interrupting contemptuously and continuing.)* . . . to pacify me. To try to keep me from spiting him. *(To the DIRECTOR.)* Yes—do as she asks—because it's true. I enjoy it immensely—because the more she begs, the more she tries to work her way into his heart. And the more aloof he holds himself, the more distant he becomes. What a joke!

DIRECTOR: Are we starting the second act or not?

STEPDAUGHTER: I won't say anymore. But you can't play the whole thing in the garden as you suggested.

DIRECTOR: Why not?

STEPDAUGHTER: Because he's *(Indicating the SON again.)* always in his room with the door locked. And then there's the rôle of that poor, confused little boy. It all takes place indoors.

DIRECTOR: Yes. I know that. On the other hand, I can't stick up little signs telling the audience where the scene takes place—*or* change sets three or four times in one act.

MALE LEAD: They did once . . .

DIRECTOR: Yes, when the audience was as naïve as that little girl there.

FEMALE LEAD: It's the simplest kind of illusion.

FATHER: *(Jumps up, disturbed.)* Illusion? Don't use that word. Please. You have no idea how cruel we find it!

DIRECTOR: *(Astounded.)*. Cruel? Why?

FATHER: Yes! Cruel! Cruel! You should understand that!

DIRECTOR: Then what should we say? We meant the illusion that we have to create—here—on stage—for our audience.

MALE LEAD: Through our acting.

DIRECTOR: The illusion of a reality.

FATHER: I understand, sir—but perhaps you can't understand *us*. Excuse me—for you and the actors all this is just a game. And well it should be.

FEMALE LEAD: *(Interrupting him, indignant.)* Game?! We're not children! We take our work seriously!

FATHER: I don't deny that. And I expect from the play of your art—as this gentleman just said—the illusion of reality.

DIRECTOR: Right.

FATHER: Just consider that for us *(Indicates the other FIVE CHARACTERS.)* there is no reality outside of this illusion.

DIRECTOR: *(Looks at his equally stupefied ACTORS.)* And what does all that mean?

FATHER: *(After watching them all, with a wan smile.)* Of course. What else can there be? For you an illusion is something you have to create. For us it's our sole reality. *(Brief pause. He takes a few steps toward the DIRECTOR.)* But not only for us. Just think about it. *(He looks into his eyes.)* Can you tell me who you are? *(Stands there, pointing at him.)*

DIRECTOR: *(Perplexed, a half-smile on his lips.)* What? Who I am? I'm me.

FATHER: And what if I said that's not true—because you are me?

DIRECTOR: I'd tell you that you were crazy.

(The ACTORS laugh.)

FATHER: Yes. Laugh. You're quite right. Because everything here is a game. *(To the DIRECTOR.)* And you can object that it's only in the spirit of play that that gentleman there *(Indicates the MALE LEAD.)*, who is unquestionably himself, must be me, who, on the contrary, am unquestionably myself. The one you see here. As you can see, I've caught you in a trap.

(The ACTORS laugh again.)

DIRECTOR: *(Annoyed.)* We've been through this once. Must we do it again?

FATHER: No—no—that's not what I meant. I would like you to abandon this game . . . *(Looking at the FEMALE LEAD as if to prevent what she is about to say.)* this game of art. Of *art!* The game you and your actors play regularly—here—in this theater. And therefore I ask you once again: Who are you?

DIRECTOR: *(Turning to the ACTORS, astonished and irritated).* The nerve! He comes in calling himself a stage character, and asks me who I am!

FATHER: *(With dignity, but not haughtily.)* A stage character, sir, may always ask a person who he is. Because a stage character has a life of his own. Marked by his own unique characteristics. That's why he is always somebody.

Whereas a person . . . and I don't mean you specifically . . . a person in general can very well be nobody.

DIRECTOR: Wonderful! But you're asking *me*—the *director*—the *boss!* Understand?

FATHER: *(Softly, with gentle humility.)* But only to know if you, as you are now, see yourself as you once were. In some distant past. With all the illusions that were once yours. All the things, inside and out, as they appeared to you then. As they indeed were for you then. Well, sir. Think back on those illusions—that you no longer have. On all of those things that no longer seem what they once were for you. Don't you feel that the very . . . I won't say boards of this stage . . . no . . . but the earth itself . . . is slipping away from under you? That the you that you feel yourself to be today, that all your reality as you know it now . . . is destined tomorrow to seem to you a mere illusion?

DIRECTOR: *(Without having understood much, but astonished by the specious argument.)* Yes—well—just what are you trying to say?

FATHER: Nothing. Except to make one thing clear. If *we (Indicating the other CHARACTERS.)* have no other reality than illusion, then you might question your *own* reality. The reality you breathe and live. Because just like yesterday's reality, today's reality is destined tomorrow to be an illusion.

DIRECTOR: *(Deciding to make fun of him.)* Marvelous! In other words, you and this play of yours are more true and more real than I am.

FATHER: *(Totally serious.)* Without a doubt, sir. Yes!

DIRECTOR: Oh?

FATHER: I thought you understood that from the beginning.

DIRECTOR: More real—than I am?

FATHER: If your reality can change from one day to the next . . .

DIRECTOR: But we know that—we know it can change—it's always changing. Like everybody else's.

FATHER: *(With a cry.)* Not ours! No! Don't you *see!* That's the *difference!* Our reality *doesn't* change! It *can't* change! It can *never* be different! It's *fixed!* As it *is! Forever!* It's terrible. This immutable reality. It should make you shudder when you come near us.

DIRECTOR: *(Parries quickly with an idea that has just occurred to him.)* Excuse me. Explain to me, please. When has a stage character ever stepped out of his rôle and done what you have done? When? Tell me. It's new to me.

FATHER: It's new because authors keep the secrets of their creation to themselves.

When living characters stand before him, he has no choice but to follow the words and movements that they suggest to him. Otherwise there's trouble. The moment a character is born, he's independent of his author. He can be imagined in a whole host of situations that his author never considered. And at times this character becomes infinitely more important than his author ever dreamed.

DIRECTOR: Yes. I know all that.

FATHER: Then why are you so astonished to see us here? Imagine the misfortune. A character is born of an author's imagination. An author who then tries to deny him life. Tell me, does this character . . . left unfulfilled in this way . . . alive, yet without a life . . . have the right to do what we are now doing? Here? In front of you? We've spent an eternity—an eternity—trying to convince him, to urge him, to realize us. First I, then she *(Indicates the STEPDAUGHTER.)*, then her poor mother would present ourselves to him . . .

STEPDAUGHTER: *(Comes forward as if in a trance.)* It's true. I too. I too. I too would go and tempt him. In the melancholy silence of his study. At twilight. To tempt him. He sat in his chair. Unable to decide to turn on a light. Letting the room grow darker. Darker. Around him. Till the room, the darkness, trembled with our presence. *(As if she sees herself in that study and is bothered by the presence of the ACTORS.)* Oh, why can't you go away! Why can't you leave us alone! Mama! There! With her son! I and the little girl! The boy! There! Always alone!—And then! He *(With a slight gesture to indicate the FATHER.)* and I . . . ! And then me! Alone! Alone in this darkness! *(A sudden movement, as if she wanted to take hold of the living and luminous vision of herself that she sees emerging from the gloom of the study.)* Yes! My life! What scenes! What wondrous scenes! Suggested to him! I! I tempted him! More than the others!

FATHER: Yes, maybe it was your fault. You were too insistent . . . too impudent . . .

STEPDAUGHTER: What? But he made me that way. *(Approaches the DIRECTOR; confidentially.)* I think he was disillusioned—with the theater—with the public that makes the theater what it is.

DIRECTOR: Can we get on with this? Let's go! Let's get to the action!

STEPDAUGHTER: Action? I thought we had too much. I mean, once we enter his house . . . *(Indicates the FATHER.)* You're the one who said you couldn't put up signs or change the set every five minutes.

DIRECTOR: That's right. We can't. We have to combine the action into a continuous well-knit scene. Your way is impossible. Your brother can't come home from school and wander around like a ghost from room to room—brooding out a plan—behind closed doors. That makes him . . . what did you say?

STEPDAUGHTER: Wither—shrivel up—completely . . .

DIRECTOR: Well . . . whatever. And you could see it in his eyes.

STEPDAUGHTER: Yes. Look at him. *(Indicates the BOY beside the MOTHER.)*

DIRECTOR: And at the same time you want the little girl playing—unaware—in the garden. The boy in the house—the girl in the garden. Right?

STEPDAUGHTER: Yes, in the sun, happy. It's my only pleasure. Her happiness, her joyousness—there—in the garden—freed of the misery, of the squalor, of that horrible room where all four of us slept together. And I had to sleep with her. Me—with her. Think of it! My contaminated body next to hers—next to that child! And she would wind her dear innocent little arms around me. Press me to her. Whenever she saw me, in the garden, she ran to me, took me by the hand. She didn't care about the big flowers. She sought out the tiny little ones. She would show them to me.—And she was so happy . . . so happy! *(Overwhelmed by the recollection, she bursts out in a long, despairing cry. Her head drops onto her arms on the table. Everyone is moved. The DIRECTOR goes over to calm her.)*

DIRECTOR: *(In an almost fatherly voice.)* Don't worry. We'll have it in the garden. You'll be pleased. We'll play it all in the garden. *(He calls a STAGEHAND by name.)* Fly in a couple of trees. Two small cypresses—over there—in front of the fountain.

(Two small cypresses are lowered from the fly-space. The CREW HEAD goes over to secure them.)

DIRECTOR: *(To the STEPDAUGHTER.)* This is only to give you an idea. *(He again calls the STAGEHAND by name.)* Give me some sky!

STAGEHAND: *(From the flies.)* Can't hear!

DIRECTOR: *(Loudly so as to be heard.)* A sky backdrop! Behind the fountain! *(A white drop is lowered.)* No! Not white! A sky! Never mind. It'll do. I'll take care of it. *(Calling.)* Whoever's on lights. Turn everything off. I need some atmosphere. Give me some blues on the white drop. Moonlight. There you go. Great.

(The scene is bathed in a mysterious moonlight effect. The ACTORS, affected by the mood, move and speak as though actually in a moonlit garden.)

DIRECTOR: *(To the STEPDAUGHTER.)* There. You see? Now the boy, instead of hiding behind doors inside, can run around the garden. Hide behind the trees. But finding a small girl won't be easy. For the scene where she shows you the flowers, you know? *(To the BOY.)* Come here a minute. Let's see what we've got here. *(When the BOY doesn't move.)* Well, come on. *(He pulls him forward and tries to make him hold his head erect, but each time it falls back down.)* Off to a good start, I see. What's the matter with him? Why doesn't he talk? *(Putting his hand on the BOY's shoulder, he leads him behind one of the cypresses.)* Come on. Come over here. Now. I want you to hide behind one of these trees. There. That's right. Stick your head out now—like you're spying. *(He steps back in order to get a view of the effect as the BOY goes through the action. The ACTORS are both dismayed and affected by what they see.)* Wonderful! Wonderful! *(To the STEPDAUGHTER.)* What if the little girl saw him peeking out? She could run over. Maybe get him to say something.

STEPDAUGHTER: *(Rises.)* He won't say a word. Not as long as he's *(Indicating the SON.)* here. You'll have to send him away first.

SON: *(Goes resolutely to one of the flights of steps leading into the auditorium.)* Gladly. Couldn't suit me better. What more could I want?

DIRECTOR: *(Quickly holding him back.)* No! Where do you think you're going? Come back here!

(The MOTHER rises, filled with anguish at the thought that he will leave. She instinctively raises her arms to prevent him, without ever leaving her place.)

SON: *(Has reached the edge of the stage, to the DIRECTOR who is restraining him).* I'm not involved in this! Let me go! Please! Let me go!

DIRECTOR: What do you mean you're not involved?

STEPDAUGHTER: *(Calmly, ironically.)* Don't worry about him. He won't leave.

FATHER: He has to play that terrible scene—with his mother—in the garden!

SON: *(Suddenly, resolutely, fiercely.)* I'm not playing anything! I told you that! At the start! Let me go!

STEPDAUGHTER: *(Running over to them, to the DIRECTOR.)* Please? Allow me? *(She releases his hold of the SON.)* Let him go. *(To the SON.)* All right. Go!

(The SON stands as if frozen at the steps. As if held by some mysterious power, he cannot descend. Then, with the ACTORS looking on in bewilderment, he walks slowly along the edge of the stage to the other flight of steps. But he freezes there, too, however much he wants to go down them. The

STEPDAUGHTER, *who has watched him intently and with unspoken challenge, bursts out laughing.)*

STEPDAUGHTER: He can't! Do you see? He can't! He has no choice! He's chained to us! Indissolubly! But if I, if I run away! If I run away when what is inevitable happens! If I run away!! Only because I hate him! Because I hate the sight of him! Well! If I'm still here! If I can still endure the sight of him! The presence of him! How can he run away? How can he, who has to stay here, run away? Has to stay here! With his precious father! With his mother! There! Who without him has no more children! *(To the MOTHER.)* Come, Mama! Come! *(To the DIRECTOR, indicating the MOTHER.)* There. You see? She got up. To stop him. *(To the MOTHER, as if motivating her by some magic power.)* Come. Come. *(To the DIRECTOR.)* You can imagine how ashamed she is. To show these actors of yours what she really feels. But her desire to be with him is so great that she's ready . . . ! Look. You see? She's ready to live out her scene with him . . .

(And, in fact, the MOTHER has gone up to her SON, and as the STEP-DAUGHTER speaks her last words, the MOTHER makes a gesture to indicate that she consents.)

SON: *(Quickly.)* No! No! Not me! If I can't leave, I'll stay. But I won't, I won't act out anything!

FATHER: *(To the DIRECTOR, excitedly.)* You can force him!

SON: No one can force me!

FATHER: I'll force you!

STEPDAUGHTER: Wait! No, wait! First the little girl has to go to the fountain. *(She rushes over to the LITTLE GIRL, kneels in front of her and takes her face in her hands.)* My poor little love. You look so bewildered. Your beautiful little eyes. Asking where you are. We're on a stage, dear. What's a stage? Why, it's a place where you play at being serious. They put on plays here. And now we're going to put on a play. Yes. We really are. And you, too. *(She embraces the LITTLE GIRL, presses her to her and rocks her for a time.)* Oh, my dear . . . my love . . . what a terrible play for you . . . what a horrible ending they've made up for you. The garden—the fountain—it's all make-believe, of course. The terrible thing is, everything's make-believe here. But maybe you'll like a make-believe fountain to play by—even better than a real one. Mm? But no. For the others it will be a game. But not for you. Alas. Because you're real. And you really play by a real fountain. Big—beautiful—green—with lots of bamboo shoots casting shadows, reflecting in the water. And little baby ducklings swimming around, breaking up the shadows. You try to catch one—one of the ducklings . . . *(With a scream that terrifies everyone.)* No, Rosetta, no! Your mama's not watching you! Because of that bastard of a son! And my head feels like it's full of devils! And that one—there. *(She leaves the LITTLE GIRL and turns with her usual contempt to the BOY.)* What are you hanging around here for? You with your stupid little beggar's face! It's your fault, too, when that baby drowns! All you do is hang around! As if I didn't pay for everyone when I brought you into this house! *(She grabs his arm to force him to take his hand out of his pocket.)* What have you got there? What are you hiding? Show me your hand. *(She pulls his hand out of his pocket and discovers, to everyone's horror, that it is clenched around a revolver. She looks at him for a moment with a degree of satisfaction, then says somberly.)* Hm. Where did you get that? *(When the BOY, frightened, his eyes wide open, does not reply.)* Idiot! If I had been you, I wouldn't have killed myself! I'd have killed one of them! Or both of them! Father and son together! *(The STEPDAUGHTER pushes him back behind the cypresses where he has been hiding. She then takes the LITTLE GIRL and lowers her into the fountain until she is no longer visible. She then kneels beside the fountain and lowers her head onto her arms on the fountain's rim.)*

DIRECTOR: That's it! Now . . . *(Turning to the SON.)* both at the same time!

SON: *(Scornfully.)* What do you mean? Both at the same time! It's not true! There never was a scene between me and her! *(Indicating the MOTHER.)* Let her tell you how it happened!

(The SECOND FEMALE LEAD and the JUVENILE LEAD at this point separate themselves from the group of ACTORS. She observes the MOTHER with great care, and he the SON, both of them rôles they will eventually have to act.)

MOTHER: Yes. It's true. I did go into his room.

SON: Into my room! Understand? Not the garden!

DIRECTOR: That's not important. As I've said. We have to shift the action into a single scene.

SON: *(Noticing that the JUVENILE LEAD is studying him.)* What do you want?

YOUNG ACTOR: Nothing. Just looking at you.

SON: *(Turning around to face the SECOND FEMALE LEAD.)* Ah! So you're here, too! Studying to play her rôle?

DIRECTOR: Yes! Exactly! And I suggest you show some gratitude! For their interest!

SON: Ah! Thank you very much! But hasn't it occurred to you yet? You'll never be able to stage this piece. There isn't a fragment of us in any of you. Your actors study us from the outside. Life can't be lived in front of a mirror—a mirror that throws back frozen images of ourselves—frozen expressions—twisted into some horrible grimace!

FATHER: That's true! He's right! Don't you see that?

DIRECTOR: *(To the JUVENILE LEAD and the SECOND FEMALE LEAD.)* That's fine. Go back with the others.

SON: It's useless! Leave me out of it!

DIRECTOR: Just be quiet! Let me listen to your mother. *(To the MOTHER.)* So. You went into him.

MOTHER: Yes. Into his room. I couldn't stand it anymore. I wanted to empty my heart of the anguish that tormented me. But the minute he saw me enter . . .

SON: There was no scene! I left! I left because I didn't *want* a scene! I never had a scene with her! Understand?

MOTHER: That's true. That's how it was—how it was.

DIRECTOR: But we *have* to have a scene between you and him. It's essential.

MOTHER: I'm ready, sir. Anytime. Please! If there's a chance. Let me talk to him. I want to pour out to him all that's in my heart!

FATHER: *(Going to the SON, in a rage.)* You'll do it! For your mother! Your mother!

SON: *(More determined than before.)* I won't do anything!

FATHER: *(Taking hold of him and shaking him.)* My God! Will you listen! Will you listen! Don't you hear her? Don't you have a heart?

SON: *(Grabbing the FATHER.)* No! No! Let's end this! Once and for all! *(General agitation. The MOTHER tries to come between them to separate them.)*

MOTHER: Please! Please!

FATHER: *(Without letting loose of him.)* Listen to me! Listen!

SON: *(After a brief struggle, and to the horror of all present, he throws the FATHER to the ground near the steps.)* Are you crazy? Haven't you any decency? Parading your shame here in front of the world! *And* ours! I want nothing to do with it! Nothing! I stand for the will of our author in this! The author who didn't *want* to put us on the stage!

DIRECTOR: But you came here asking . . .

SON: *(Indicates the FATHER.)* He did! Not me!

DIRECTOR: And *you?* Aren't *you* here?

SON: *He* wanted to come! He dragged us all with him! And now the two of you get together and decide to show not only what *did* happen, but what *didn't!*

DIRECTOR: Then tell me what *did* happen! *Tell* me! You left the room without a word . . .

SON: *(After a brief hesitation.)* Without a word . . . because I didn't want there to be a scene . . .

DIRECTOR: *(Urgently.)* And then? What did you do then?

SON: *(With everyone watching him in anguished anticipation, he takes a few steps.)* Nothing . . . walking in the garden . . . *(Breaking off, he becomes gloomy and absorbed.)*

DIRECTOR: *(Moved by his reserve, urges him to continue.)* And? What happened . . . walking in the garden . . .

SON: *(Embittered, buries his head in his arms.)* Why do you force me to say this? It's horrible!

(The MOTHER trembles violently and with stifled sobs looks toward the fountain.)

DIRECTOR: *(Slowly noticing the direction of the MOTHER's glance, he turns toward the SON with mounting apprehension.)* The little girl?

SON: *(Staring straight ahead, directly into the auditorium.)* There . . . in the fountain . . .

FATHER: *(Still on the floor, pointing with tender pity at the MOTHER.)* She was following him . . .

DIRECTOR: *(Anxiously to the SON.)* And you?

SON: *(Slowly, staring straight ahead.)* I rushed over . . . to pull her out . . . Then suddenly I stopped . . . frozen.—I saw something. Behind the trees. The boy—the boy—standing there—unmoving. His eyes—wild—looking over—at the fountain . . . at his drowned sister. *(The STEP-DAUGHTER is bent over the fountain, hiding the LITTLE GIRL. Her sobbing comes like an echo from the background. Pause.)* I wanted to go to him. And then . . . *(From behind the trees where the BOY is hiding comes the sound of a revolver shot.)*

MOTHER: *(With an anguished cry she and the SON along with the ACTORS rush over to the fountain.)* My child! My boy! *(Then, amid the general confusion and individual cries, she screams.)* Help! Help!

DIRECTOR: *(Trying to clear a space amid the shouting, while the BOY is carried off behind the white drop.)* Is he wounded? Is he really hurt?

(All, except for the DIRECTOR and the FATHER, who is still on the floor near the steps, have disappeared behind the white drop. We hear their murmured

cries and exclamations. After a moment they return from behind both sides of the drop.)

FEMALE LEAD: *(Coming from the right, grieved.)* He's dead! The poor thing! He's dead! Oh, my God!

MALE LEAD: *(Coming from the left, laughing.)* Dead! It's a game! A game! Don't believe it!

OTHER ACTORS: *(Coming from the right.)* Game? It's real! It's real! He's dead!

OTHER ACTORS: *(Coming from the left.)* No! It's a game! It's all a game!

FATHER: *(Rises and cries out.)* No! It's not a game! It's real! It's real! Real! *(In desperation he disappears behind the white drop.)*

DIRECTOR: *(At the end of his endurance.)* Game! Reality! You can all go to hell! Lights! Lights! Lights!

(The stage and the auditorium are suddenly flooded with brilliant light. The DIRECTOR breathes freely again as if having been released from a nightmare. They all stand and look at each other in an attitude of suspense and dismay.)

DIRECTOR: Good God!! What the hell was that all about! We lost a whole damned day on their account! *(Looks at his watch.)* You can go. All of you. Not much more we can do here today. Too late to start a rehearsal. See you this evening. *(After the ACTORS have all gone off with various good-byes, to the Electrician.)* Hey! Whoever's on lights! Turn everything off! *(He has scarcely finished his words than the theater is plunged into total darkness.)* Jesus Christ! Give me at least *one* light to see my way out!

(Suddenly, as if by accident, a green floodlight comes on behind the drop, projecting enormous silhouettes of the CHARACTERS—minus the BOY and the LITTLE GIRL—onto the drop. The DIRECTOR, terrified, leaps from the stage. At the same moment, the green floodlight is switched off and the stage is again bathed in blue. Slowly, the SON emerges from the right side of the drop, followed by the MOTHER, her arms outstretched toward him. The FATHER then comes from the left. They stop center stage as if caught in a dream. Finally the STEPDAUGHTER emerges from the left and runs down to one of the flights of steps into the auditorium. She stops suddenly on the first step, turns, looks back at the three others, and breaks into strident laughter. She then dashes down the steps into the auditorium and runs up the aisle. She turns again, laughs, looking at the three figures left behind on the stage. She leaves the auditorium, her laughter still heard resounding in the corridors. After a brief moment the curtain falls.)

END OF PLAY

Henry IV

(Enrico IV)

1922

CAST OF CHARACTERS

Henry IV
The Marchesa Matilda Spina
Frida *her daughter*
Carlo Di Nolli *the young Marquis*
The Baron Tito Belcredi
Doctor Dionysius Genoni

THE FOUR MAKE-BELIEVE PRIVY COUNSELORS
Landolph (Lolo)
Harold (Franco)
Ordulph (Momo)
Berthold (Fino)

Giovanni *the old servant*
Two Pages *in costume*

SCENE

An isolated Italian country villa in Umbria during the 1920s.

Henry IV

ACT ONE

The great hall in the villa. It has been carefully decorated to resemble the throne room of Henry IV in the imperial palace at Goslar. Among all the antique furnishings two large, modern, life-size oil portraits stand out. They hang on the wall at the rear, a slight distance from the floor and on a carved wooden ledge that runs the length of the wall. The ledge protrudes far enough from the wall to serve as a bench for anyone who might want to sit. One portrait is at the left and the other at the right of the throne with its low baldacchino midway in the wall's length, dividing the protruding ledge. The portraits are of a man and a women, both of whom are young and dressed in carnival costumes, the male as Henry IV, the female as Matilda of Tuscany. When the curtain rises, the two PAGES leap as if surprised from the ledge on which they are lying and take up their positions, along with their halbards, on either side of the foot of the throne as if they were statues. After a few seconds, HAROLD, LANDOLPH, ORDULPH, and BERTHOLD enter through the second exit on the right. They are all young men who are paid by the MARQUIS CARLO DI NOLLI to play the rôles of Privy Counselors, which is to say vassals of the lower aristocracy, at the court of Henry IV. They are dressed, therefore, like German knights of the eleventh century. The last one in, BERTHOLD, whose real name is Fino, is new to the job and just beginning his first day. His three companions who are showing him the ropes are at the same time amusing themselves at his expense. The scene is to be played rapidly and with particular vivacity.

LANDOLPH: *(To BERTHOLD as if in the process of explaining something to him.)* And this is the throne room.
HAROLD: At Goslar.
ORDULPH: Or, if you prefer, at the castle in the Hartz.
HAROLD: Or at Worms.
LANDOLPH: According to which scene we're called upon to be involved in, you'll be kept jumping around with us from one place to another.
ORDULPH: Saxony!
HAROLD: Lombardy!

LANDOLPH: The Rhine!

FIRST PAGE: *(Unmoving except for his lips.)* Psst! Psst!

HAROLD: Yes?

FIRST PAGE: *(Rigid as a statue, sotto voce; referring to Henry IV.)* Is he coming or isn't he?

ORDULPH: No. He's asleep. Take it easy.

> *(Both PAGES relax. The SECOND PAGE, releasing a sigh of relief, goes to lie down again on the ledge.)*

SECOND PAGE: Jesus! At least you could have told us!

FIRST PAGE: *(Going to HAROLD.)* Got a light?

LANDOLPH: Sorry, no pipes.

FIRST PAGE: Relax, it's a cigarette.

> *(HAROLD offers him a light and he goes to lie down on the ledge. BERTHOLD meanwhile has been looking things over in a state somewhere between admiration and bewilderment.)*

BERTHOLD: Excuse me . . . but this room . . . these costumes . . . I don't understand. Which Henry IV are we talking about? The French one or . . . ?

> *(LANDOLPH, HAROLD, and ORDULPH burst out laughing, with LANDOLPH pointing at BERTHOLD, urging the others to carry the ragging even further.)*

LANDOLPH: Ha! Listen to him! French!

ORDULPH: He thought he was the French one!

HAROLD: German! Henry IV of Germany! Salic dynasty and all that!

ORDULPH: The great and tragic Emperor!

LANDOLPH: Henry IV of Canossa! We're forever waging the terrible war between Church and State!

ORDULPH: Empire against papacy!

HAROLD: Anti-popes against pope!

LANDOLPH: Kings against anti-kings!

ORDULPH: War against Saxons!

HAROLD: And all the rebel princes!

LANDOLPH: Even against the Emperor's own sons!

BERTHOLD: *(Protects his head with his hands against this avalanche of information.)* All right! All right! I get it! No wonder! It was all wrong! The costumes, the room! People didn't dress this way in the sixteenth century! I was right, then!

HAROLD: Sixteenth century! Hell!

ORDULPH: We're smack in the middle of the eleventh!

LANDOLPH: Figure it out. It's January 25, 1071, and we're outside Canossa.

BERTHOLD: *(More bewildered than ever.)* Jesus! I sure screwed that up!

ORDULPH: Sure did! Even worse if you thought you were at the French court!

BERTHOLD: All the history I buried myself in!

LANDOLPH: We've got four hundred years' jump on you, kid. You aren't even in diapers yet.

BERTHOLD: *(Getting angry.)* Shit! At least they could have told me he was the German one! They gave me two weeks to bone up! Oh, God, and all the books! And for what?!

HAROLD: But you must have known you were taking Tito's place—and Tito played Adalbert of Bremen.

BERTHOLD: Adalbert! Hell! I wasn't told a thing!

LANDOLPH: No, look—I mean, when Tito died, the Marquis di Nolli—

BERTHOLD: He's the one, all right! Damn! He could have told me!

HAROLD: Probably thought you knew.

LANDOLPH: He didn't want to hire another Tito. Thought the three of us would do. But then he began shouting: "They've driven out my Adalbert—" because for him, you see, poor Tito wasn't dead. To him he was Bishop Adalbert who'd been driven out of court by the rival Bishops of Cologne and Mainz.

BERTHOLD: *(Grabbing his head with both hands.)* I don't know what you're talking about!

ORDULPH: All the worse for you, I'd say!

HAROLD: What's worse, even we don't know who you're supposed to be.

BERTHOLD: You what? Not know who . . . ?

ORDULPH: Hm! Well! Berthold, I suppose.

BERTHOLD: All right, so I'm Berthold! Just who *is* this Berthold and why am I supposed to be playing him?

LANDOLPH: "They've driven out my Adalbert," he shouted, "so now I want Berthold, I want Berthold!"

HAROLD: Berthold? Berthold who? Don't ask us!

ORDULPH: Then suddenly here you are! Berthold!

LANDOLPH: And a great job you'll do, too!

BERTHOLD: *(Objecting and on the verge of leaving.)* No! Sorry! Not me, thank you very much! I'm gone! Out of here!
(HAROLD and ORDULPH restrain him and pull him from the door while the others laugh.)

HAROLD: Easy, there! Easy! Calm down!

ORDULPH: Any chance you're the Berthold of fairy tale fame?

LANDOLPH: Don't worry about it. We don't know who we are, either. He's Harold, he's Ordulph, and I'm Landolph. It's what he calls us. We're used to it. But who are we really? Period names. Just like yours—a period name. Berthold! Only one of us, poor Tito, was given a really great part to play. Even history knows who he is. Bishop of Bremen. He looked the rôle, too. Played it to a T.

HAROLD: He read up on his character every free moment.

LANDOLPH: He even went around ordering His Majesty about. Took him in charge, guided him like a regular tutor, counseled him. We're counselors, too, when you get down to it. Privy Counselors, of course, and that's about it. And why? Because history tells us that Henry IV was hated by the upper aristocracy for surrounding himself at court with young men of the lower classes.

ORDULPH: Which is us.

LANDOLPH: Right! Insignificant royal small fry. Devoted, a bit dissolute, good-humored.

BERTHOLD: Must I be good-humored, too?

HAROLD: You said it, kid! Just like us.

ORDULPH: Take my word for it, it's no picnic.

LANDOLPH: It's a real pity, you know? What more do we need? It's all here. Think of the production we could throw together with all these historical costumes. We'd have them beating down the doors to get at it! Audiences go wild over things like that these days. Jesus, we've got enough material for a dozen plays! All of them about Henry IV! But here the four of us are—and those two over there when they're on duty! *(Indicates the PAGES.)* And what do we do? Zero. No director. No scenes. Shit! I mean, we're all form and no content. Worse off, if you ask me, than the *real* Henry's *real* privy counselors. No one gave *them* a rôle to play; but of course they didn't need one; they played themselves, their real lives. They played their rôle because they played their rôle. Looked out for their own interests and the hell with anyone else. Sold investitures and God knows what else. And here we are, stuck in this magnificent court—all dressed up with nothing to do! Six puppets hanging on a wall, waiting for some master to come along, get them on their feet and say something!

HAROLD: Bull! What do you mean "nothing to do"? What we have to do is give him the right answer when he asks! Hit the nail on the head! No fudging. Fail in that and your ass has had it!

LANDOLPH: Yes, well, you're right, I guess.

BERTHOLD: Oh, that's just fine! Right answers? How? I've been boning up on the French Henry and *he's* the German one! Ah?
(LANDOLPH, ORDULPH, and HAROLD laugh.)
HAROLD: Get a move on, kid. You've got a lot of lost time to make up for.
ORDULPH: Don't sweat it. We'll help.
HAROLD: We've got a mountain of books on the subject in there. A quick run-through'll get you by for a while.
ORDULPH: You'll catch on.
HAROLD: Look! *(He turns him around and shows him the portrait of the MARCHESA MATILDA on the back wall.)* Now who do you think she might be?
BERTHOLD: *(Looking.)* Her? Well, first of all, I'd say she's a bit out of place. Two modern paintings surrounded by all this respectable antiquity?
HAROLD: Right. Fact is, they weren't meant to be there. Behind each of them there's a niche. Meant for period-style statues. But they changed their mind, and now those paintings hide them.
LANDOLPH: *(Interrupting and continuing.)* They'd be more than out of place if they were only paintings.
BERTHOLD: So what are they if not paintings?
LANDOLPH: Well, sure, if you go touch them, they're paintings. But for him—*(Makes a mysterious gesture to the right, meaning Henry IV.)* who *doesn't* touch them . . .
BERTHOLD: So what are they to him?
LANDOLPH: Just guessing, you know, but I think I'm pretty much on track. They're images—images like, well—like those a mirror throws back at you. Know what I mean? That one there, over there—*(Points at the portrait of Henry IV.)* is Henry as he is today, alive in this throne room, which also happens to be—as is only proper—in the style of the period. Why does that surprise you? I mean, if you were standing in front of a mirror, how would you see yourself? You'd see yourself alive, here, now, dressed in medieval costume. Mmn? All right. Now. Imagine those paintings two mirrors reflecting living images. Images, here in the midst of a world that—that—that you'll see come alive for yourself. And it will, don't worry, you'll see. You'll be living here with us. You'll see it all.
BERTHOLD: Just for the record, I'd like to say that . . . that I have no intention letting this job drive me nuts!
HAROLD: Nuts! Hell! You'll enjoy it!
BERTHOLD: Where'd you learn all this?

LANDOLPH: You don't time-travel eight hundred years without *something* rubbing off.

HAROLD: Let's go! We're wasting time. You'll get the knack of it.

ORDULPH: Be sopping it up before you know it.

BERTHOLD: Good! Let's get to it! First the basic facts.

HAROLD: Trust us. We're in this together.

LANDOLPH: When we're through with you, you'll be a top-of-the-line puppet! Let's go! *(Takes him by the arm to lead him off.)*

BERTHOLD: *(Stopping and looking at the portrait on the wall.)* No, wait, hold on! Who is she? You haven't said. The Emperor's wife?

HAROLD: The Emperor's wife is Bertha of Susa, sister of Amadeus II of Savoy.

ORDULPH: And the Emperor, who wants to be young along with us, can't stand her and wants her out of the way. Divorce, you know?

LANDOLPH: *(Indicating the portrait.)* She's his fiercest enemy: Matilda, Marchesa of Tuscany.

BERTHOLD: Right! The one who played host to the pope . . .

LANDOLPH: There you go! At Canossa!

ORDULPH: Pope Gregory VII.

HAROLD: Our bugaboo, no less! Come on, let's go!
(All four move toward the right exit by which they entered, when the door at the left opens and the old servant, GIOVANNI, enters in evening dress.)

GIOVANNI: *(Quickly, anxiously.)* Oh! Psst! Franco! Lolo!

HAROLD: *(Stopping and turning.)* What is it?

BERTHOLD: *(Astonished at seeing him enter the throne room in evening dress.)* Well! What's this? What's *he* doing here?

LANDOLPH: A man of the twentieth century? Out! Off with you!
(They rush over to him, including the two PAGES, pretending to menace him and throw him out.)

ORDULPH: He's an emissary of Gregory VII! Out!

HAROLD: Out! Out of here! Go!

GIOVANNI: *(Defending himself, annoyed.)* Stop all this, I say! Stop it!

ORDULPH: No! You're not allowed in here!

HAROLD: Get out! Out!

LANDOLPH: *(To BERTHOLD.)* It's magic is what it is! A demon conjured up by the Sorcerer of Rome! Draw, draw your swords! *(Makes a move as if to draw his sword.)*

GIOVANNI: *(Shouting.)* Stop it, do you hear! Stop this fooling! The Marquis has arrived with a number of his friends . . .

LANDOLPH: *(Rubbing his hands.)* Ah! First rate! Any women?

ORDULPH: Old? Young?

GIOVANNI: There are two gentlemen.

HAROLD: But the women! Who are the women?

GIOVANNI: The Marchesa and her daughter.

LANDOLPH: *(Astonished.)* What?!

ORDULPH: The Marchesa?!

GIOVANNI: The Marchesa! The Marchesa!

HAROLD: And the gentlemen?

GIOVANNI: I don't know.

HAROLD: *(To BERTHOLD.)* They've come to bring us the content we lack! You'll see!

ORDULPH: Emissaries of Gregory VII! Ah! What fun!

GIOVANNI: Will you let me finish!

HAROLD: Be our guest.

GIOVANNI: I'd say one of the two gentlemen is a doctor.

LANDOLPH: Oh, God, not another!

HAROLD: Bravo, Berthold! You'll bring us luck!

LANDOLPH: We'll give this doctor a run for his money!

BERTHOLD: I'd say I've landed myself in a real pickle!

GIOVANNI: Listen to me, will you? They want to come in here.

LANDOLPH: *(Astonished and puzzled.)* What? Her? The Marchesa? Here?

HAROLD: I suspect we're in store for a bit more than content!

LANDOLPH: Here's where the tragedy begins.

BERTHOLD: *(Curious.)* Tragedy? Why?

ORDULPH: *(Pointing at the portrait.)* Because she's the one who posed for that portrait.

LANDOLPH: Her daughter is the fiancée of the young Marquis di Nolli.

HAROLD: But why are they here? Would someone enlighten me?

ORDULPH: If *he* sees her, all hell will break loose.

LANDOLPH: He may not recognize her after all this time.

GIOVANNI: If he wakes up, I'd advise keeping him in there.

ORDULPH: Is that some kind of joke?

HAROLD: You know what he's like!

GIOVANNI: Then use force! That's an order! Now go!

HAROLD: All right! All right! Let's hope he's not awake yet.

ORDULPH: Right! All right! We're going! We're going!

LANDOLPH: *(As he starts off with the others, to GIOVANNI.)* I trust you'll tell us later what all this means?

GIOVANNI: *(Shouting after them.)* Lock the door after you, and hide the key! And that door, too! *(Indicating the other door on the right.)*
(LANDOLPH, HAROLD, ORDULPH, and BERTHOLD leave by the second door on the right.)

GIOVANNI: *(To the two PAGES.)* Out! You, too! That way! *(Pointing at the first door on the right.)* Lock the door after you and hide the key.
(The two PAGES leave as directed. GIOVANNI goes to the door on the left and opens it to admit the MARQUIS DI NOLLI.)

DI NOLLI: Have you given them their orders clearly?

GIOVANNI: Yes, my lord. You needn't worry.

(DI NOLLI goes out again for a moment to invite the others in. The first to enter the room are BARON TITO BELCREDI and DOCTOR DIONYSIUS GENONI, followed by LADY MATILDA SPINA and the young MARCHESA FRIDA. GIOVANNI bows and goes out. LADY MATILDA SPINA is about forty-five, still beautiful and shapely, although there are ample signs that she has tried to repair the inevitable ravages of time with makeup, causing her head to resemble that of a Valkyrie. This makeup assumes a prominence that contrasts with and severely disturbs her mouth which is both very beautiful as well as sad. A widow for many years, she has taken as her friend the BARON TITO BELCREDI, a man neither she nor anyone else ever takes seriously—or at least so it seems. What TITO BELCREDI really means to her he alone knows, making it possible, therefore, for him to laugh if she pretends not to know herself. In any event, he can always laugh at the laughter that the jokes she makes at his expense give rise to in the others. Slim, prematurely gray, and somewhat younger than she, his head is curiously bird-like. He would be a most lively individual if the supple agility that makes him a formidable swordsman were not, so to speak, sheathed in a sleepy, Arab-like languor that reveals itself in his nasal and drawling voice. FRIDA, the MARCHESA's daughter is nineteen. Overshadowed by her imperious and too-conspicuous mother, she is affected in her obscurity by the facile gossip provoked by the latter, gossip that is directed equally at herself. She has the good fortune, however, to be engaged to the MARQUIS CARLO DI NOLLI, a rigid young man, most indulgent where others are concerned, but closed and fixed in regard to what he believes he amounts to in the world, though at bottom it is possible that not even he really knows. In any event, he is dismayed by all of the responsibilities he feels are weighing him down, and feels that the others, bless them all, have every right to gossip away at will and to enjoy themselves, but not he; not because he wouldn't like to, but because he simply isn't able. He is dressed in strict

mourning for the recent death of his mother. DOCTOR DIONYSIUS GENONI has the rubicund and impudent face of a satyr, with bulging eyes, a short pointy little beard that shines like silver; his head is nearly bald and he has good manners. They enter in a state of consternation, as if afraid, and look around the room—except for DI NOLLI—at first speaking in low voices.)

BELCREDI: Ah, magnificent! Magnificent!

DOCTOR: How very interesting! Even the surroundings reflect his insanity. Everything just right. Magnificent! Yes, yes, magnificent!

LADY MATILDA: *(Has been looking around for her portrait; spotting it, she moves closer to it.)* Ah, there it is! *(Admiring it from the right distance, she expresses mixed feelings.)* Yes . . . yes . . . Oh, look . . . My God . . . *(To her daughter.)* Frida, Frida . . . Look . . .

FRIDA: Ah, your portrait?

LADY MATILDA: No! Look! It's not me! It's you!

DI NOLLI: It's true! I told you so!

LADY MATILDA: But I could never have believed you! *(Shaking as if from a chill down her spine.)* God, what a feeling! *(Then looking at her daughter.)* Come, Frida. *(Pulling her close, she puts an arm around her waist.)* Don't you see yourself in me, there?

FRIDA: Well, I . . . I'm not . . .

LADY MATILDA: You don't see the resemblance? But how is that possible? *(Turning to BELCREDI.)* Tito, you look. Tell her.

BELCREDI: *(Without looking.)* No-no-no, I won't look! For me the answer is no—*a priori.*

LADY MATILDA: How stupid! You think you're paying me a compliment! *(Turning to the DOCTOR.)* Speak up, Doctor! Say something.
(The DOCTOR makes a movement in the direction of the portrait.)

BELCREDI: *(With his back turned, pretending secretly to call him back.)* Psst! No, Doctor! For God's sake, stay out of it!

DOCTOR: *(Bewildered and smiling.)* But why shouldn't I?

LADY MATILDA: Pay him no attention! Come, now. He's insufferable!

FRIDA: He's a professional fool. Didn't you know?

BELCREDI: *(To the DOCTOR as he sees him going over.)* Watch your feet, watch your feet, Doctor, your feet!

DOCTOR: My feet? But why should I?

BELCREDI: You're wearing hob-nailed boots!

DOCTOR: I am?

BELCREDI: Absolutely! Be careful you don't crush four delicate glass feet.

DOCTOR: *(Laughing loudly.)* Nonsense! Why should I—what's so surprising about a daughter resembling her mother . . .

BELCREDI: Ba-boom! He's done it now!

LADY MATILDA: *(With exaggerated anger, advancing toward BELCREDI.)* What is it? What's he done? What's he said?

DOCTOR: *(Innocently.)* Well, isn't that true?

BELCREDI: *(Answering the MARCHESA.)* He said there's no reason to be surprised, and yet you appear terribly surprised. But why, when it's all so natural to you now?

LADY MATILDA: *(Even angrier.)* What a fool you are! What a silly fool! Can't you see it's because it *is* so natural? Because it *isn't* my daughter up there? *(Points at the canvas.)* That's *me* up there, a portrait of *me,* and to find my daughter in it was an amazing experience, amazing—and my amazement was genuine, gentlemen, genuine, and don't you ever cast doubts upon that! *(After this violent outburst there is a moment of awkward silence.)*

FRIDA: *(Softly, annoyed.)* Dear God, always the same. Always arguments over nothing.

BELCREDI: *(Also softly, as though with his tail between his legs, apologetically.)* I cast no doubts upon anything. I simply noticed from the start that you didn't share your mother's amazement. Or if you did, it was because the resemblance between you and the portrait was so great.

LADY MATILDA: Of course. She refuses to recognize herself in me as I was at her age. And yet I recognize myself in her as she is at this moment.

DOCTOR: How true! A portrait is a moment of time forever frozen. For the young lady it is free of associations and memories; while for her mother the Marchesa it is filled with memories of everything: movements, gestures, glances, smiles, not to mention many other things that aren't even in the portrait . . .

LADY MATILDA: Exactly! There you are!

DOCTOR: *(Continuing, turning toward her.)* And it's only natural that you should see them alive here in your daughter.

LADY MATILDA: He spoils every innocent pleasure—every moment of spontaneous sentiment. And for no other reason than to infuriate me.

DOCTOR: *(Dazzled by the light he has thrown on the situation, turns to BELCREDI, adopting his professional tone.)* Resemblance, dear Baron, is frequently the result of imponderables. Which accounts for the fact that—

BELCREDI: *(Cutting short the lecture.)* —that it might also be possible to find a resemblance between the two of us, my dear professor!

DI NOLLI: Can we put an end to this, please! *(Pointing to the two doors on the right as if to warn that someone might be listening.)* We've wasted enough time as it . . .

FRIDA: Indeed we have! That happens when he's . . . *(Indicating BEL-CREDI.)*

LADY MATILDA: Precisely why I didn't want him with us.

BELCREDI: But when you've had so much fun at my expense? What ingratitude!

DI NOLLI: That will be enough, thank you, Tito! The Doctor is here, and we've come on some very serious business that is of great importance to me.

DOCTOR: Exactly. Let's first try to get at some facts. This portrait of you, Marchesa, excuse me, but how did it come to be here? Did you give it to him?

LADY MATILDA: No, no. How could I have given it to him then? I was just like Frida—except I wasn't engaged. I gave it to him three or four years after the accident. I gave it to him at the urgent insistence of his mother. *(Indicating DI NOLLI.)*

DOCTOR: Who happened to be his sister? *(Indicating the doors on the right, alluding to Henry IV.)*

DI NOLLI: Yes, Doctor. It's a debt—our coming here, that is—that we owe to my mother who died a month ago. Otherwise we—she and I *(Indicating FRIDA.)* would be away on a trip . . .

DOCTOR: And thinking of quite other matters. I understand.

DI NOLLI: She died with the firm conviction that her adored brother was well on the way to recovery.

DOCTOR: And what signs, if I may ask, led her to this conclusion?

DI NOLLI: Certain strange remarks he made to her not long before mother died.

DOCTOR: Strange remarks. Mm. I see. It would help greatly, of course, to know precisely what they were.

DI NOLLI: No, I'm afraid not. All I know is that she returned from her last visit with him very upset. It appears he displayed uncharacteristic tenderness toward her that in a way forecast her approaching death. On her deathbed she made me promise never to neglect him; that I would have doctors visit and check him . . .

DOCTOR: Aha. Well, good. Let me see, now, let me see . . . It often happens, you see, that even the slightest causes . . . Well, this portrait, for example . . .

LADY MATILDA: Really, now, Doctor, I see no sense in attaching all this importance to it. It struck me as it did only because I hadn't seen it in years.

DOCTOR: Excuse me, please . . . just one moment . . .

DI NOLLI: She's absolutely right, you know, Doctor. It must have been there for at least fifteen years . . .

LADY MATILDA: No, no, more! At least eighteen by now!

DOCTOR: Excuse me, but you really don't know yet what I'm trying to get at! I place great importance, very great, I may say, on these two portraits, painted, if I'm not mistaken, before the famous—mm, most unfortunate—cavalcade. Am I correct?

LADY MATILDA: Yes. Yes, of course.

DOCTOR: Which was, of course, while he was perfectly in control of his senses—and that is precisely what I've been trying to get at. Was it he who suggested that they be painted?

LADY MATILDA: No, Doctor, no. Several of us who took part in the cavalcade had them done—as a kind of memento of the event.

BELCREDI: I had one done, too—as Charles of Anjou!

LADY MATILDA: As soon as the costumes were ready.

BELCREDI: Because it was suggested, you see, that they all be hung together in a gallery of the villa where the cavalcade took place—as a remembrance. As it turned out, everyone wanted to keep his own.

LADY MATILDA: Mine here, as I've already said, I gave to him—without, in fact, much regret—because his mother . . . *(Again indicating DI NOLLI.)*

DOCTOR: Do you know whether or not *he* requested it?

LADY MATILDA: No, I'm afraid I don't. Possible, though . . . Or perhaps his sister . . . to encourage the love affair . . .

DOCTOR: Just one other thing, one thing more. Was the cavalcade his idea?

BELCREDI: *(Quickly.)* Oh, no, Doctor, no, it was mine!

DOCTOR: Please . . .

LADY MATILDA: Pay him no attention. It was poor Belassi's.

BELCREDI: Belassi!!

LADY MATILDA: *(To the DOCTOR.)* Count Belassi, who died, poor thing, two or three months later.

BELCREDI: But Belassi wasn't even there when . . .

DI NOLLI: *(Annoyed at the threat of another discussion.)* Excuse me, Doctor, but is it imperative we establish whose idea it was?

DOCTOR: Yes, well, it would certainly help me to . . .

BELCREDI: But the idea was mine, all mine! Oh, this is unbelievable! Not that I have anything to be proud of because of it, considering the outcome. Look, Doctor—I remember exactly how it happened. I was in the club one night early in November, looking at an illustrated magazine— German, as it turned out, just for the pictures, since I don't read German. One of the pictures was of the Emperor in one university town or another where he'd been a student.

DOCTOR: Bonn, Bonn.

BELCREDI: Yes, Bonn, that was it, Bonn. He was on horseback and decked out in one of those strange traditional costumes worn by German student guilds in medieval times. Following him was a procession of other students of the nobility, also on horseback and in costume. And that's where I got it, the idea, from that picture. At the club, you see, we were considering putting on a grand pageant during the coming carnival season. And so I proposed this historical cavalcade. Well, historical in a fashion—actually more Tower of Babelish, if you know what I mean. We were each to impersonate a historical character from this or that century: king, emperor, prince—and beside him on horseback, his lady, queen, empress, as the case may be. The horses, of course, were also fitted out in the style of the period. And so—my proposal was accepted.

LADY MATILDA: My invitation came from Belassi.

BELCREDI: It's embezzlement is what it is, if he says the idea was his! He wasn't even *at* the club the night I proposed it! And neither was *he!* *(Alluding to Henry IV.)*

DOCTOR: And he chose the character of Henry IV?

LADY MATILDA: Yes. And allowing my own name to make the choice, I said I'd come as the Marchesa Matilda of Tuscany.

DOCTOR: I'm . . . afraid I don't grasp the connection . . .

LADY MATILDA: Yes, well, neither did I at first. He told me that from that time forward he would be at my feet like Henry IV at Canossa. I knew about Canossa, of course—but to be honest, I really didn't have a firm grasp on the history. And I remember the odd impression I had as I did research to prepare for my part. I discovered that I was the loyal and zealous friend of Pope Gregory VII, who at the time was locked in a fierce conflict with the Emperor of Germany. I then understood why he wanted to be near me in that cavalcade: I'd chosen to play his implacable enemy.

DOCTOR: Ah, perhaps because . . .

BELCREDI: Oh, for heaven's sake, Doctor! It was because at the time he was furiously paying court to her, and she, naturally . . .

LADY MATILDA: *(Pointedly, with fire.)* Naturally! Naturally! Nothing natural about it!

BELCREDI: *(Pointing at her.)* There! You see? She couldn't stand him!

LADY MATILDA: No, that's not true! It wasn't at all that I couldn't stand him! On the contrary! It's just that when a man wants to be taken seriously . . .

BELCREDI: *(Continuing.)* He gives you indelible proof of his stupidity.

LADY MATILDA: No, dear heart, not in this case. He wasn't nearly as stupid as you.

BELCREDI: When have I *ever* asked to be taken seriously!

LADY MATILDA: How right you are! But with him there was no joking. *(In a different tone, turning to the DOCTOR.)* One of the many misfortunes of being a woman, Doctor, is suddenly to find a pair of eyes staring at you with the intense promise of eternal devotion! *(She bursts out in high-pitched laughter.)* There's nothing more ridiculous! If only men could see themselves with that look of eternal fidelity in their faces! It's always sent me into fits of laughter. Then even more than now. But I have a confession to make. I can do so now after twenty years and more. When I laughed at him . . . it was also partly out of fear. One might almost have believed such a promise from eyes like his. And that would have been very dangerous.

DOCTOR: *(With lively interest, concentrating.)* Ah, yes . . . well . . . I see! This . . . this is most interesting—most interesting, indeed! But why very dangerous?

LADY MATILDA: *(Lightly.)* Because he wasn't like the others. And also because . . . well . . . I'm—I'm . . . what shall I say . . . *(Looking for an unpretentious word.)* impatient—there we are—impatient with everything that is formal and boring. But I was young then, you see, so young and . . . and a woman. I was champing at the bit; but had to control myself. It would have required more courage than I felt I had. And so, I laughed at him, too. But not without remorse. Not without disgust for myself. For laughing at him the same way as the others. All those stupid people. Making fun of him.

BELCREDI: Not unlike my own case, more or less.

LADY MATILDA: People laugh at you, my dear, because of that look of fake humility you dress in. It was quite different with him. And what's more, people laugh in your face.

BELCREDI: Better than behind my back, at any rate.

DOCTOR: Shall we—shall we get back to the subject? I gather from what you say that even at the time he was already . . . shall we say—eccentric?

BELCREDI: Yes, but in a very odd way, Doctor.

DOCTOR: How?

BELCREDI: Well . . . I suppose you could say . . . cold-bloodedly . . .

LADY MATILDA: Cold-bloodedly? If he was odd, Doctor—and there's no question about that—it was because he was full of life! He was an original!

BELCREDI: I'm not saying he was faking his eccentricity. On the contrary, he was often genuinely eccentric. But I swear, Doctor, that he was aware—totally aware—of the eccentricity he was performing—as though he suddenly saw himself from outside. And I'm also certain he suffered because of it. He was so furious with himself at times that he was actually comic.

LADY MATILDA: That's very true!

BELCREDI: *(To LADY MATILDA.)* And why? *(To the DOCTOR.)* Because I think he would have felt that moment of instant lucidity that an actor experiences when performing a rôle. The moment that suddenly puts him out of touch with his own feelings, which seemed to him—if not exactly false, because he *was* sincere—but something he immediately felt the need to . . . how should I say . . . to . . . to intellectualize—to compensate for the sincere and heartfelt warmth that he felt he lacked. And so he improvised, exaggerated, let himself go—in order to . . . to distract himself from his own troubles . . . to forget himself. To others he would appear inconsistent, fatuous, and—well . . . to be quite honest . . . ridiculous.

DOCTOR: And . . . would you say, unsociable?

BELCREDI: No, not at all! He was known for organizing tableaux vivants, dances, benefit recitals—just for the fun of it, you understand. But he was also a quite good actor, you know.

DI NOLLI: And since his madness he's become quite a brilliant one! Terrifying.

BELCREDI: Yes, but at the start, too. Just imagine, when the accident happened and he fell from the horse . . .

DOCTOR: Fell on his head, I believe . . .

LADY MATILDA: Oh, it was horrible! He was right beside me! I saw him lying there between the horse's hoofs just as it was rearing . . .

BELCREDI: At first, of course, no one thought he'd hurt himself seriously.

The cavalcade had stopped because of the confusion, and people wanted to know what had happened. But by that time he'd been taken back to the villa.

LADY MATILDA: Nothing! Nothing at all! Not even a scratch! Not a drop of blood.

BELCREDI: We thought he'd only fainted . . .

LADY MATILDA: And then, about two hours later, when . . .

BELCREDI: Yes, when he reappeared again in the main room of the villa . . . that's just what I was going to say . . .

LADY MATILDA: The look on his face! I knew at once!

BELCREDI: No! That's not true! We realized nothing! Not one of us! Believe me, Doctor!

LADY MATILDA: Well, of course *you* didn't! You were all running around acting like lunatics!

BELCREDI: Nonsense! We were acting out our rôles! It was an absolute Babel!

LADY MATILDA: Well, you can imagine, Doctor, the shock when we realized that he was taking his part seriously.

DOCTOR: Ah, so that by that time he, too, had . . .

BELCREDI: Yes! Joined us! Right in our midst! We all thought he'd recovered and begun acting with the rest of us—better, in fact! I told you what a splendid actor he was. What could we think but that he was joking?

LADY MATILDA: Some of them in fun began lashing at him with their whips . . .

BELCREDI: Well, then . . . he was armed, you see—as any king would be—and he drew his sword and began brandishing it at two or three of us! It was terrifying! Just terrifying! For all of us!

LADY MATILDA: I'll never forget that scene. Our masked faces, hideous and distorted, looking at the awful mask of his face, which was no longer a mask, but madness itself!

BELCREDI: Henry IV! Henry IV to the life! And in a moment of rage!

LADY MATILDA: For more than a month, Doctor, he obsessed over that masquerade, made it a part of everything he did. It must have affected him.

BELCREDI: He studied, he studied hard for the rôle, no detail too many . . .

DOCTOR: Well, then, that explains it! A blow to the head with consequent damage to the brain, transformed a momentary obsession into a permanent fixation—fixed in perpetuity. Such accidents can cause mental unbalance, or even madness.

BELCREDI: *(To FRIDA and DI NOLLI.)* And so, my dears, you can see the jokes life plays on us. *(To DI NOLLI.)* You were four or five when it happened. *(To FRIDA.)* And your mother fancies that you've taken her place there in that portrait, when, in fact, at the time, she hadn't the slightest inkling that she would be bringing you into the world. In the meantime, I've grown gray, and he—look at him! *(Pointing at the portrait.)* Pow! One knock on the head and he's Henry IV for ever and ever, amen!

DOCTOR: *(Has been lost in thought, now spreads wide his fingers in front of him as if to draw attention to himself, and prepares to deliver his scientific explanation.)* What it comes down to, ladies and gentlemen, is this . . . *(Suddenly the downstage right door bursts open admitting a very angry BERTHOLD whose face appears transformed, and who is barely able to control himself.)*

BERTHOLD: *(Rushing in.)* I'm sorry. I beg your pardon . . . *(He stops suddenly when he is aware of the confused amazement his entry has caused.)*

FRIDA: *(Shouting in terror, seeking protection.)* Oh, God! There he is!

LADY MATILDA: *(Retreating in fear, one arm covering her face to avoid seeing him.)* Is it him? Is it him?

DI NOLLI: *(Quickly.)* Of course it's not him! No! Calm down!

DOCTOR: *(Astonished.)* Who the hell is it, then?

BELCREDI: One of our renegade masqueraders!

DI NOLLI: One of four young men we keep here to help him in his madness.

BERTHOLD: I beg your pardon, Marquis . . .

DI NOLLI: Damn your pardon! I gave strict orders that all doors were to be locked and no one admitted!

BERTHOLD: Yes, Signore! But I can't take much more! I'm asking your permission to leave!

DI NOLLI: Yes, I see, you're the new one. You were to begin work here this morning.

BERTHOLD: Yes, Signore, and I'm telling you I can't . . .

LADY MATILDA: *(To DI NOLLI with consternation.)* I don't understand. You said he was perfectly calm.

BERTHOLD: *(Quickly.)* Oh, no, madam, no! He's not the problem! It's my companions! You said, Signore, they were here to help. But they're not here to help, at all! They're the mad ones! I walk in here this morning for the first time, and instead of helping me, they . . . *(LANDOLPH and HAROLD make an excited appearance in the same doorway at the right, but stop before entering.)*

LANDOLPH: With your permission . . .

HAROLD: With your permission, Marquis . . .

DI NOLLI: Oh, come in, for heaven's sake! What is all this? What's the meaning of . . .

FRIDA: Oh, God! I'm getting out of here! I'm afraid! *(She begins moving toward the left exit.)*

DI NOLLI: *(Restraining her at once.)* No, Frida, don't!

LANDOLPH: My lord, this idiot here . . . *(Indicates BERTHOLD.)*

BERTHOLD: *(Protesting.)* Thanks anyway, but this idiot's had it! I'm out of here!

LANDOLPH: What do you mean, you're out of here!

HAROLD: He's ruined everything, Signore, running off here!

LANDOLPH: It's thrown him into a rage in there! We can't keep him in there much longer! He ordered his arrest, and insists on passing sentence on him at once—from the throne! What do we do?

DI NOLLI: You start by closing the door! Close it! Now!

(LANDOLPH goes to close the door.)

HAROLD: Ordulph can't possibly manage him on his own in there . . .

LANDOLPH: What if we announce your arrival at once, my lord? It might help to distract him. Have the gentlemen decided how they want to be presented?

DI NOLLI: Yes, yes, it's all been arranged. *(To the DOCTOR.)* If you think it's wise to examine him immediately, Doctor . . .

FRIDA: No, not me, no, Carlo! I'm leaving! And you, too, mother, for heaven's sake! Come with me! Come!

DOCTOR: Do you think . . . he isn't armed, is he?

DI NOLLI: Of course he's not armed! Really, Doctor! *(To FRIDA.)* I'm sorry, Frida, but this fear of yours is quite childish! After all, you did want to come!

FRIDA: Oh, no, not me! It was mother!

LADY MATILDA: *(Firmly.)* And I'm ready to see him. So what do we do?

BELCREDI: Really, now, is it necessary to disguise ourselves that way?

LANDOLPH: Indispensable, Signore! Absolutely indispensable! Unfortunately! As you can see . . . *(Indicating his own costume.)* There'd be hell to pay if he saw you in modern dress.

HAROLD: He'd think it was some diabolical disguise.

DI NOLLI: Just as they look disguised to you, we'd appear in disguise to him in the clothes we're wearing.

LANDOLPH: It might not matter at all if he didn't suppose it was the work of his mortal enemy.

BELCREDI: Pope Gregory VII?

LANDOLPH: Exactly! He calls him a "pagan"!

BELCREDI: The pope? That's a good one!

LANDOLPH: Yes, Signore. And that he raises the dead. And practices black magic. He's terrified of him.

DOCTOR: A persecution complex.

HAROLD: He'd start raving.

DI NOLLI: *(To BELCREDI.)* There's really no need for you to be there, you know. Only the Doctor. We can wait outside.

DOCTOR: What are you saying? I go in alone?

DI NOLLI: You won't be alone. These three will be with you.

DOCTOR: No, no . . . I mean, if the Marchesa . . .

LADY MATILDA: Of course I'll be there. It's why I came. I want to see him again!

FRIDA: But why, mother? Please! Do come with us!

LADY MATILDA: *(Imperiously.)* I will do exactly as I please! Why else have I come? *(To LANDOLPH.)* I shall be "Adelaide," the mother.

LANDOLPH: Ah! Excellent! The mother of the Empress Bertha! Good! In that case, the Marchesa need only wear the ducal crown, and a mantle to cover the rest. *(To HAROLD.)* Off you go, Harold!

HAROLD: Yes, but what about the gentleman? *(Indicating the DOCTOR.)*

DOCTOR: Ah, yes . . . I think we decided the Bishop . . . Bishop Hugh of Cluny.

HAROLD: I think it's Abbot you mean, Signore. Abbot Hugh of Cluny.

LANDOLPH: He's been here frequently before . . .

DOCTOR: *(Astonished.)* What's that? He's what?

LANDOLPH: You needn't worry. All I meant is, it's an easy disguise.

HAROLD: We've used it often before.

DOCTOR: But . . .

LANDOLPH: He'll never remember. He's more interested in the costume than the person in it.

LADY MATILDA: That will do just as well for me, too, then.

DI NOLLI: We're leaving, Frida. You come too, Tito.

BELCREDI: No. If she stays *(Indicating the MARCHESA.)* I stay.

LADY MATILDA: But I really don't need you.

BELCREDI: Need me or not, I want to see him. I'd enjoy it. And you say I'm not allowed?

LANDOLPH: Actually, you know, it would be better if there were three.

HAROLD: And the gentleman's costume?

BELCREDI: Oh, just anything that isn't too complicated.

LANDOLPH: *(To HAROLD.)* Yes, probably something from Cluny, too.

BELCREDI: Cluny? What would that be?

LANDOLPH: A Benedictine habit of the Abbey of Cluny. You'll be in attendance on the Monsignore. *(To HAROLD.)* Off you go! *(To BERTHOLD.)* And you, too—and don't let him see you the rest of the day! *(But as soon as he sees them coming.)* No, wait. *(To BERTHOLD.)* You bring back the clothes he'll *(Indicating HAROLD.)* give you. *(To HAROLD.)* And you go immediately and announce the arrival of the "Duchess Adelaide" and "Monsignore Hugh of Cluny." Understand? *(HAROLD and BERTHOLD go off through the first door to the right.)*

DI NOLLI: All right, then, we'll withdraw. *(He and FRIDA leave through the door at the left.)*

DOCTOR: *(To LANDOLPH.)* I dare say he'll look favorably on me dressed as Hugh of Cluny.

LANDOLPH: Yes, you can be certain of that. The Monsignore has always been received here with the greatest respect. And you, too, Marchesa. You may rest assured. He's never forgotten that after two days of being kept waiting in the snow, nearly frozen to death, it was at the intercession of the two of you that he was admitted to the Castle of Canossa and the presence of GregoryVII, who at the time didn't want to receive him.

BELCREDI: Excuse me, and what do I do?

LANDOLPH: You will stand respectfully to the side, Baron.

LADY MATILDA: *(Irritated and very nervous.)* Go away altogether would be better!

BELCREDI: *(Peevishly, in a low voice.)* You've certainly got yourself into a state . . .

LADY MATILDA: *(Proudly.)* I am as I am! Just leave me in peace!
(BERTHOLD returns with the clothing.)

LANDOLPH: *(Seeing him enter.)* Ah! Here we are with the costumes! This mantle for you, Marchesa!

LADY MATILDA: Just a moment, I'll take off my hat. *(She removes it and hands it to BERTHOLD.)*

LANDOLPH: Take it over there. *(To the MARCHESA as he offers to place the ducal crown on her head.)* May I?

LADY MATILDA: Oh, dear, isn't there a mirror around anywhere?

LANDOLPH: Why, certainly. Over there. *(Indicates the door at the left.)* If the Marchesa would prefer doing it herself . . .

LADY MATILDA: Yes, I think it would be better. Give it here. I'll only be a second. *(She takes back her hat and goes out with BERTHOLD who carries the mantle and crown. Meanwhile, the DOCTOR and BELCREDI set about putting on their Benedictine robes the best they can without help.)*

BELCREDI: I must confess, I never expected to end up a Benedictine monk. By the way, this little insanity of his must be costing a bundle!

DOCTOR: Yes, insanity doesn't come cheap.

BELCREDI: But of course when you've got a fortune to go with it . . .

LANDOLPH: Yes, Signore! We have an entire wardrobe over there. Period costumes every one of them. Copied to perfection from antique garments. It happens to be my specialty around here. I buy only from the very best theatrical costumiers. It's not inexpensive.

(LADY MATILDA returns wearing the crown and mantle.)

BELCREDI: *(Quickly, admiring her.)* Ah, magnificent! Truly regal!

LADY MATILDA: *(Seeing BELCREDI, bursts out in laughter.)* Oh, God! No-no, take it off! You're impossible! You look like an ostrich decked out as a monk!

BELCREDI: Well, look at the Doctor!

DOCTOR: Oh, never mind . . . never mind . . .

LADY MATILDA: No, the Doctor's quite all right . . . but you drive me into hysterics!

DOCTOR: *(To LANDOLPH.)* Do you have many such receptions?

LANDOLPH: That depends. Every once in a while he'll order someone or other to appear before him, which means, of course, that we have to go out scouting for someone able to play the part. That goes for women, too.

LADY MATILDA: *(Hurt but trying to conceal the fact.)* Ah, really! Women, too!

LANDOLPH: Yes . . . many at first.

BELCREDI: *(Laughing.)* Oh, that's marvelous! In costume? *(Indicating the MARCHESA.)* Like that?

LANDOLPH: Yes, well, you know . . . the kind of women who . . .

BELCREDI: The kind of women who . . . I understand. *(In a nasty tone to the MARCHESA.)* Be careful, you're entering dangerous waters!

(The second door on the right opens and HAROLD enters. He first gestures inconspicuously for all conversation to cease, then announces solemnly.)

HAROLD: His Majesty the Emperor!

(The two PAGES enter first and assume their positions at the foot of the throne. Then, flanked by ORDULPH and HAROLD, who walk a respectable distance behind him, HENRY IV enters. He is close to 50, very pale looking, with gray hair already at the back of his head. At the temples and in front his hair appears blond, the result of a puerile and very obvious tinting. On each cheek, amid all that tragic pallor, is a doll-like daub of red, also very obvious. Over his royal regalia he wears a penitent's sackcloth, as at Canossa. His eyes are fixed with a look of suffering that is terrible to see, a look that is at odds with the attitude of one who is working hard to appear humbly repentant, while at the same time letting the world know that the humiliation is anything but deserved. ORDULPH holds the imperial crown in both hands, while HAROLD carries the royal scepter with the eagle and the globe with the cross.)

HENRY IV: *(Bowing first to LADY MATILDA, then to the DOCTOR.)* Madam . . . Monsignore . . . *(He then sees BELCREDI and is on the verge of bowing to him as well, but turns instead to LANDOLPH, who has approached him, and asks diffidently in a low voice.)* Is this Peter Damiani?

LANDOLPH: No, Your Majesty, he's a monk from Cluny attending on the Abbot.

HENRY IV: *(Turns again to observe BELCREDI with mounting diffidence, and noticing that he keeps looking with uncertainty and embarrassment at LADY MATILDA and the DOCTOR, as if seeking advice, draws himself upright and shouts.)* It *is* Peter Damiani! And it's quite useless, Father, to look at the Duchess! *(Turning quickly to LADY MATILDA as though to ward off a danger.)* I swear to you, my lady, I swear, that my heart has changed toward your daughter! I confess that if he *(Indicating BEL-CREDI.)* hadn't come in the name of Pope Alexander to forbid it, I would have repudiated her! Oh, believe me, yes, there were those ready to uphold me in the divorce. The Bishop of Mainz, for one. He would have done it for one hundred and twenty plots of farmland. *(Looks a bit perplexed at LANDOLPH and adds quickly.)* But I shouldn't be speaking badly about the bishops at a time like this. *(Returns humbly to BEL-CREDI.)* Believe me, I am grateful, profoundly grateful for the impediment you imposed. My life is a series of humiliations—my mother, Adalbert, Tribur, Goslar—and now this sackcloth you see me dressed in. *(His tone of voice suddenly changes and he speaks like someone reviewing his rôle in an astute parenthesis.)* It's not important. Clarity of mind, perspicacity, firmness of attitude, and patience in adversity. These are what matter. *(Turning to everyone and speaking solemnly.)* I know how to correct the errors I am guilty of, and I can even humble myself before you, Peter Damiani. *(Bowing deeply, he remains in that curved position as if bent by an oblique suspicion that is born in him, compelling him, as if against his will, to add in a threatening tone.)* Unless, of course, it was you who began the obscene rumor that my sainted mother, Agnes, was having illicit relations with the Bishop of Auguste?

BELCREDI: *(While HENRY IV remains bent over, with an accusatory finger pointing at him, he places both his hands on his chest in denial.)* No, not me, never!

HENRY IV: *(Straightening up.)* Not true, then? No? Infamy! *(Looking at him awhile, adds.)* I didn't think you capable of it. *(He approaches the DOCTOR and tugs at his sleeve with a sly wink.)* It's always "them" who are to blame, eh, Monsignore? Always the same.

HAROLD: *(Softly, in a whisper, as if prompting.)* Eh, yes, those rapacious bishops.

DOCTOR: *(To HAROLD, trying to stay in character.)* Yes, oh, them . . . of course . . . yes . . .

HENRY IV: Nothing ever satisfies them. I was a poor young lad, Monsignore . . . passing the time, playing, even, and never suspecting I was king. I was six when I was torn from my mother, six, Monsignore, and they used me against her, I knowing nothing, used me even against the power of the dynasty, profaning everything, stealing, stealing, each greedier than the other, Anno more than Stephen, Stephan more than Anno.

LANDOLPH: *(Softly, persuasively, to rebuke him.)* Your Majesty . . .

HENRY IV: *(Turning quickly.)* Ah, yes, of course! This is hardly the time to speak ill of the bishops. But this infamous, this libelous accusation against my mother, Monsignore, is more than can be endured. *(He looks at the MARCHESA and grows tender.)* And I can't even weep for her, my lady. But you have a mother's heart. I know. And so I appeal to you. A month ago now, she came to see me, all the way from her convent. They told me that she's dead. *(Long, emotional pause, then with a sad smile.)* I can't weep for her, you see . . . because if you are here, and I'm like this . . . *(Shows his sackcloth.)* then I'm only twenty-six years old.

HAROLD: *(Almost whispering, gently, to comfort him.)* Which means that she's alive, Your Majesty.

ORDULPH: And still in her convent.

HENRY IV: *(Turning to face them.)* Yes, how true, and I can put off my grief to another time. *(Almost coquettishly he brings the MARCHESA's attention to the tint he has used on his hair.)* You see? Still a blond . . . *(Then softly, as if in confidence.)* This is for you. I don't need it, of course. But a little exterior touching up does no harm. A matter of age, Monsignore, if you catch my drift. *(Drawing close to the MARCHESA, he observes her hair.)* Ah, and I see that . . . you, too, Duchess . . . *(He winks and gestures expressively with his hand.)* Italian, um? *(As if saying: fake: but with no sign of contempt, but, rather, mischievous admiration.)* God forbid I should show disgust or surprise. Impossible dreams. Which of us admits to the inscrutable and fatal power that sets limits to the will? But, you see, if one is born and one dies . . . You, Monsignore, did you want to be born? I didn't. And between both extremities, between birth and death, and quite independent of our will, so many things happen that we wish had never happened, that we resign ourselves, however reluctantly, to the admission of our own powerlessness!

DOCTOR: *(Speaking only to cover the time needed to study him attentively.)* Yes . . . yes . . . all too true . . . unfortunately . . .

HENRY IV: There it is, you see? Refuse to be resigned and out creep our desires. A woman wants to be a man . . . an old man wants to be young again . . . None of us lies. None of us pretends. What else is there to say? We have all, genuinely and unshakably, convinced ourselves that our splendid conception of ourselves is the one, the only, and the true one. And yet, Monsignore, while you stand firm in your faith, your hands clinging tightly to your holy cassock, something slips slowly down your sleeves, slithering like a snake escaping its skin, something of which you haven't the slightest inkling. Life, Monsignore! Life! And what a surprise to see it there suddenly in front of you! Escaping, escaping . . . Spite and anger against yourself! And remorse . . . especially remorse. Ah! And that was the worst. The worst—seeing it there in front of me. The remorse! With a face I knew to be my own, and so dreadful I had to turn my eyes away . . . *(Drawing closer to the MARCHESA.)* Has it never happened to you, my lady? Have you always been the same? Never known a different person inside you? Always the same? Oh, God, but what about that day . . . what about . . . How could you have done it . . . that act . . . *(Looks so intensely into her eyes that she comes close to fainting.)* . . . yes . . . exactly . . . *that* act! I see we understand each other. And, no, I shall never reveal it to another soul. And you, Peter Damiani, how could you have been the friend of such a person . . .

LANDOLPH: *(Gently rebuking.)* Your Majesty . . .

HENRY IV: *(Quickly.)* No-no, I won't name him! I know how it upsets him.

(Turning to BELCREDI.) And what's your opinion, hm? Let's hear what you thought of him. In any case, all of us cling tightly to our conception of ourselves, the same way people growing old color their hair. What does it matter if my dyed hair doesn't deceive you? You, my lady, don't dye *your* hair to deceive others, or even yourself. You do it to deceive . . . only a little . . . a tiny, tiny bit . . . your image . . . in front of the mirror. I do it for a laugh. You do it seriously. But I assure you, no matter how serious you may be about it, you, too, are masquerading, my lady. And I don't mean the venerable crown you wear on your head, and before which I do reverence, nor your ducal robe. I refer only to that memory of yourself that you wish artificially to fix in your mind—of your lovely golden hair that one day you found so ravishing—or of your dark hair, as the case may be—the fading image of your youth. On the other hand, you, Peter Damiani, look on the memory of your past life, of what you were, of what you did, as though it were—yes, it's true, isn't it?—as if it were a dream. And so it is for me—like a dream—so many of them—inexplicable memories. Ah, well! Nothing so remarkable there, Peter Damiani. Today's life will tomorrow seem the same. *(In a sudden fit of anger, he grabs the sackcloth he is wearing.)* This sackcloth here! *(He is about to tear it off with a kind of ferocious joy when HAROLD and ORDULPH, frightened, rush to him to prevent it.)* Oh, God! *(Backing away, he removes the sackcloth.)* Tomorrow, at Bressanone, twenty-seven German and Lombard bishops, along with me, will sign the deposition warrant of Gregory VII, who is no pope, but a false friar!

ORDULPH: *(With the other two imploring him not to speak.)* Majesty! Majesty! In God's name!

HAROLD: *(Inviting him with gestures to put his sackcloth on again.)* Listen to him, Majesty!

LANDOLPH: The Monsignore is here, along with the Duchess, to intercede for you! *(Making surreptitious signs to the DOCTOR to say something quickly.)*

DOCTOR: *(Perplexed.)* Ah . . . yes . . . of course . . . we're here to intercede . . .

HENRY IV: *(Repenting immediately, and almost terrified, he allows the three to put the sackcloth back on his shoulders, and pulls it down over him with convulsed hands.)* Forgive me . . . yes . . . yes . . . forgive me, Monsignore, forgive me . . . forgive me, my lady. I feel, I swear to you, I already feel the full weight of the anathema upon me. *(He bends over, head between his hands, as if expecting something to crush him. Holding this position for a while, he then, without moving, speaks in a different voice, quietly and confidentially, to LANDOLPH, HAROLD, and ORDULPH.)* Somehow, today, and I don't know why, I can't humble myself before that one over there! *(Indicates BELCREDI with a furtive gesture.)*

LANDOLPH: *(Whispering.)* But why do you insist, Majesty, on calling him Peter Damiani, when we tell you he is not?

HENRY IV: *(Looking at him with panic fear.)* Then he isn't Peter Damiani?

HAROLD: No, Majesty, no, he's a poor monk!

HENRY IV: *(Sadly, with an exasperation of sighs.)* Ah, which of us can evaluate what he does out of instinct! Perhaps you, my lady, understand better than others, because you are a woman. This is a solemn and decisive moment. Don't you see, at this very moment, as I speak, I could accept the help of the Lombard bishops, take possession of the pope, and confine him here in the castle. I could then hurry off to Rome to elect an Anti-pope, make an alliance with Robert Guiscard, and Gregory VII would be lost! But I resist the temptation. And I am wise in that decision. I sense the spirit of the times and the majesty of one who knows how to be what he knows he must be: a pope! I suspect you feel the need to laugh at me, seeing me like this. But it would be very stupid of you. It would say that you fail to understand the political wisdom behind my wearing of these robes of penitence. Tomorrow our rôles could be reversed. And what would you do then? Laugh at the pope dressed as a prisoner? No. We would be even then. I, masquerading as a penitent today; he, tomorrow, as a prisoner. But I pity the man, king or pope, who doesn't know how to wear his mask! Perhaps just now he's a bit too cruel. Yes, that's it. Just think, my lady, think of the time when your daughter Bertha, for whom, I repeat, my feelings have changed— *(Suddenly turning to BELCREDI and shouting into his face as if he has contradicted him.)*—yes, changed, changed because of the affection and devotion she proved to me at that terrible moment! *(He stops, trembling from the burst of rage, trying to contain himself with an exasperated groan from deep in his throat. He then turns again to the MARCHESA with sweet and painful humility.)* She came with me, my lady. Down there in the courtyard now. Followed me like a beggar woman. And she's frozen. Frozen from two nights out in the snow. You're her mother. Doesn't this stir your heart to pity? Doesn't it make you want to join with him *(Indicates the DOCTOR.)* in pleading to the pope for my pardon? Pleading for him to receive us?

LADY MATILDA: *(Trembling, her voice feeble.)* Yes . . . why, yes . . . at once . . .

DOCTOR: We'll do that, yes, we'll do it!

HENRY IV: And another thing! One thing more! *(He draws them in toward him and says very softly, as if imparting a great secret.)* It isn't enough that he receive me. As you know, there's nothing he can't do—*nothing!* Even call up the dead! *(Striking his chest.)* I witness to that! I'm here! You see me! And there's no magic that he doesn't master! So, then, Monsignore, my lady—my true condemnation is this—or that—you see—*(He touches his chest, then points to his portrait on the wall as if in fear.)* forever unable to free myself from this magic. I am a penitent now and I shall remain that, I swear to you, I shall remain that until he receives me. But when the excommunication has been lifted, you, the two of you, must implore the pope to do for me that one thing that lies solely within his power: to release me from *that*—*(Points again at his portrait.)* and allow me to live this miserable life of mine freely, for he makes that impossible. One can't be twenty-six years old forever, my lady. And I also ask you this for your daughter's sake, my lady. To love her as she deserves, to love her as I now long to love her, full of tenderness as I am, made so by her pity. There . . . there you have it . . . I'm in your hands . . . *(He bows.)* My lady! Monsignore! *(Continuing to bow, he starts toward the exit by which he entered. Noticing, however, that BELCREDI, who drew closer to the group so as to hear, has turned his face to the rear, and fearing that he intends to steal the imperial crown from the throne, to the bewildered astonishment of all, he runs, snatches it, and hides it beneath his sackcloth. With a cunning smile on his lips and in his eyes, he resumes his bowing and disappears. The MARCHESA is so deeply moved that she suddenly collapses into a chair in a near-faint.)*

END OF ACT I

ACT TWO

Another room in the villa adjoining the throne room. It is furnished with austere antique furniture. To the right, about a foot and a half above the floor, there is a raised platform that resembles a choir stall. It is surrounded by a wooden banister supported by small pillars and is interrupted at the front and one side by several steps. A table and five small period chairs are situated on the platform, one at the head and two on either side. The main entrance is at the rear. Left, two windows that look out onto the garden. Right, a door to the throne room. Late afternoon of the same day. On stage are LADY MATILDA, the DOCTOR, and TITO BELCREDI. The two men are engaged in a conversation. LADY MATILDA keeps to one side, gloomy and evidently annoyed by what the two are saying. At the same time, she cannot help listening to them, because in her present agitated state of mind everything they say interests her, preventing her from developing a thought that she has just had. She listens because she instinctively feels the need to be in control of her attention at the moment.

BELCREDI: You may be right, Doctor, you may indeed be right. I was only giving you my impression.

DOCTOR: I'm not contradicting you. It's just that, well, as I said . . . an impression.

BELCREDI: Excuse me, no, he even said it . . . quite clearly. *(Turning to the MARCHESA.)* Didn't he, Marchesa?

LADY MATILDA: *(Disturbed, turning around.)* Said what? *(Then, not agreeing.)* Ah, yes . . . but not for the reason you think.

DOCTOR: He was alluding to our costumes. Your mantle *(Indicating the MARCHESA.)*—our Benedictine habits. And this is all very childish!

LADY MATILDA: *(Turning, suddenly, in anger.)* Childish? What exactly do you mean, Doctor?

DOCTOR: On the one hand, it is, yes. I beg you to allow me that, Marchesa. But on the other, it is infinitely more complicated than you can imagine.

LADY MATILDA: And yet to me it is very clear.

DOCTOR: *(With the indulgent smile that one who is competent gives to one who is not.)* Yes, well . . . we must consider the particular psychology of madmen. They notice things, you see—and quite easily, too—such as someone wearing a disguise. At the same time that they recognize the disguise, they also believe in it—like children, for whom it is both play and reality. It was in that context that I used the word *childish*. At the same time, however, it becomes extraordinarily complicated. The individual, you see, must always be totally aware of being an image to and for himself—as in that image in there. *(Alluding to the portrait in the throne room, pointing therefore to the left.)*

BELCREDI: He said so himself!

DOCTOR: There you are, you see? An image before which other images—our own—have appeared. Am I clear? And so, in his delirium, which is both acute and lucid, he at once detected a difference between his image and ours. Which is to say that our images are a pretence. He became suspicious. Madmen, you see, are constantly armed with a relentless suspicion. And that's all there is to it! We can't expect him to appreciate that *our* game is being played precisely for his own good. *His* game, on the other hand, seems all the more tragic to us because he, as if in defiance—do I make myself clear?—and induced by his suspicion, wanted to expose it as precisely the game it was. Yes, and the same can be said for him. He appeared before us with a bit of dye at his temples and on his cheeks only to be able to tell us that he had done it intentionally, as a joke!

LADY MATILDA: *(Bursting out again.)* No, Doctor! No! That's not it! That's not it at all!

DOCTOR: What is it, then, if I may ask?

LADY MATILDA: *(Vibrant with conviction.)* I am perfectly certain that he recognized me!

DOCTOR: Not possible . . . not possible.

BELCREDI: *(Simultaneously.)* Oh, really!

LADY MATILDA: *(With even greater conviction, and near to convulsion.)* But he *did* recognize me, he *did!* When he came close to speak to me, he looked into my eyes, straight into my eyes—he recognized me!

BELCREDI: But he was talking about your daughter . . .

LADY MATILDA: No! He was talking about me! Me!

BELCREDI: Well, yes, perhaps when he said . . .

LADY MATILDA: *(Letting herself go.)* About my own dyed hair! But didn't you notice how quickly he added "or of your dark hair, as the case may be"? He remembered perfectly well that in those days my hair was dark!

BELCREDI: Oh, ridiculous! Nonsense!

LADY MATILDA: *(Paying him no attention, turning to the DOCTOR.)* My hair really *is* dark, Doctor—just like my daughter's. And that's why he began to talk about her!

BELCREDI: But he doesn't know her—hasn't even seen her!

LADY MATILDA: Exactly! Why do you never understand! By my daughter he meant me! Me as I was then!

BELCREDI: Oh, this is catching, this madness—it's catching!

LADY MATILDA: *(Softly, with contempt.)* Fool!

BELCREDI: Sorry, but you were never his wife. In his delirium it is your daughter who is his wife. Bertha of Susa

LADY MATILDA: Precisely! Because I, who am no longer dark—as he remembers me—but blonde, as you see—introduced myself to him as "Adelaide," her mother. My daughter doesn't exist for him, he never saw her—as you said yourself. How would he know if she's blonde or brunette?

BELCREDI: But when he said "dark," he was only generalizing, for God's sake! As one does when trying to fix the memory of youth in the color of the hair—dark, blonde, whatever! But, true to form, you leap head-long into fantasy! You said, I believe, Doctor, that I ought not to have come! It's *she* who ought not to have come!

LADY MATILDA: *(Overcome momentarily by BELCREDI's remark, she recovers herself; then, thoughtful for a moment, insists because of her doubt.)* No . . . no . . . he was talking about *me* . . . Every word he said was spoken *to* me, *with* me, and *about* me . . .

BELCREDI: My-my-my! Talking to you all the time, was he? I dare say you didn't notice he scarcely gave me time to catch my breath! Unless you think he was alluding to you when he spoke to Peter Damiani!

LADY MATILDA: *(Defiantly, almost exceeding the limits of courtesy.)* Who knows? Then why did he take a dislike to you from the moment he saw you? To you and you alone! *(From the tone of the question the answer quite clearly is meant to be "Because he realized that you're my lover!" BELCREDI senses this as well and is left with nothing more than an empty, bewildered smile.)*

DOCTOR: I might also suggest, if I may, that only the Duchess Adlelaide and the Abbot of Cluny were announced. When a third party appeared who had not been announced, he became immediately suspicious . . .

BELCREDI: Yes, exactly! His suspicions made him take me for an enemy— Peter Damiani! She, of course, has got it in her head that he recognized her . . .

LADY MATILDA: No, there's no doubt about it! I saw it, Doctor, saw it in his eyes. That look of recognition that there is no mistaking. A split-second only, but there it was.

DOCTOR: It's certainly not to be ruled out—a single lucid moment . . .

LADY MATILDA: Yes, perhaps! Everything he said to me seemed so full— so full of regret for my youth and for his own as well—for the horrible thing that happened and that has held him prisoner in that disguise he so much wants to escape but can't.

BELCREDI: Of course! So as to be able to make love to your daughter. Or to you—as you believe—having been touched by your pity for him.

LADY MATILDA: Which, I beg you to believe, is very great.

BELCREDI: Clearly, Marchesa! So great that even a miracle-worker might attribute it to a miracle.

DOCTOR: Will you permit me my say now? Being a doctor and not a miracle-worker, I don't deal in miracles. I listened very attentively to everything he said, and I repeat that that certain analogical elasticity, characteristic to all systematized delirium, in his case appears already to be—how do I put it?—considerably relaxed. Which is to say, the elements of his delirium no longer cohere. He appears now to be in the process of slowly readjusting himself in regard to his superimposed personality—a development brought about by sudden recollections that pull him away—and this is terribly comforting—away from not a state of incipient apathy, but rather from a morbid inclination to reflexive melancholy . . . evidence, I might say, of a very considerable cerebral activity. And I repeat, it is terribly comforting. Now—and here we have it—if with this violent trick we have planned for him . . .

LADY MATILDA: *(Turning to the window, and in the lamenting tone of an invalid.)* How is it that the car is still not back? It's been three and a half hours . . .

DOCTOR: *(Stunned.)* What's that you said?

LADY MATILDA: The car, Doctor, the car! It's been more than three and a half hours!

DOCTOR: *(Taking out his watch and looking at it.)* Yes, more than four, according to this.

LADY MATILDA: It should have been back at least half an hour ago. But as usual . . .

BELCREDI: Perhaps they can't find the dress.

LADY MATILDA: But I told them exactly where it was! *(Extremely impatiently.)* But Frida . . . Where's Frida?

BELCREDI: *(Leaning slightly out of the window.)* In the garden with Carlo, I imagine.

DOCTOR: He'll talk her out of her fear . . .

BELCREDI: Not fear, Doctor. Don't you believe it. The fact is she's had it up to here.

LADY MATILDA: Do me one favor. Don't even try to convince her. I know what she's like!

DOCTOR: We'll just have to be patient. In any case, it will all be over in a second, but it must wait till evening. As I said, if we succeed in this shock tactic, if we suddenly snap all of the already weakened threads still binding him to this fiction, if we return to him what he himself asks for—he said it himself: "One can't be twenty-six years old forever, my lady."—we will be freeing him from this torment that he himself calls a torment. We will, in short, in a single blow, restore to him his sense of time—of time's passage—

BELCREDI: *(Quickly.)* He'll be cured! *(Then emphasizing each syllable ironically.)* We'll pull him out of it!

DOCTOR: —for there is hope that we can have him back again. He's like a watch that stopped at a certain hour. We stand here with that watch in hand, patiently waiting for the precise moment to come round again, and then—with a shake!—hope it will start once more and tell the correct time after so long a pause.

(At precisely this moment the MARQUIS CARLO DI NOLLI enters through the main door.)

LADY MATILDA: Oh, Carlo . . . And Frida? Where has she gone?

DI NOLLI: She's coming. She'll be here in a moment.

DOCTOR: Has the car returned?

DI NOLLI: Yes.

LADY MATILDA: Has it! And the dress?

DI NOLLI: It's been here for some time.

DOCTOR: Good! Very good!

LADY MATILDA: *(Trembling.)* Where is she? Where?

DI NOLLI: *(Shrugging his shoulders and smiling sadly, like someone who is forced against his will to take part in a bad joke.)* You'll see . . . *(Indicating the main door.)* Here she is . . .

BERTHOLD: *(Appears at the threshold of the hall and announces solemnly.)* Her Highness the Marchesa Matilda of Canossa. *(And FRIDA enters immediately, magnificent and very beautiful, dressed as the "Marchesa Matilda of Tuscany" in the dress originally worn by her mother. She is the living copy of the portrait in the throne room.)*

FRIDA: *(Passing the bowing BERTHOLD, she says with imposing condescension.)* Of Tuscany, Tuscany, if you please! Canossa is merely one of my castles!

BELCREDI: *(Admiringly.)* Just look at her, look! She's another person!

LADY MATILDA: It's me! My God, do you see her? No, Frida, stop! Do you see? My portrait come to life!

DOCTOR: Yes, yes . . . It's perfect! Perfect! The portrait!

BELCREDI: Yes, no question about it . . . exactly! Look, look! Magnificent!

FRIDA: Please don't make me laugh or I'll burst! Mother, what a tiny waist you had! I had to suck it all in before I'd fit!

LADY MATILDA: *(Nervous, fussing with the dress.)* No, no, wait . . . stand still . . . just a moment . . . these pleats . . . Is it really all that tight?

FRIDA: I'm suffocating! Let's get this over with quickly, for heaven's sake . . .

DOCTOR: But we have to wait till evening . . .

FRIDA: No, no, please, I'll never hold out till then!

LADY MATILDA: But why did you put it on so soon?

FRIDA: I couldn't help myself. The temptation! Irresistible!

LADY MATILDA: The least you could have done was call me—have asked someone to help you . . . My God, it's still all crumpled . . .

FRIDA: I know, I saw . . . but they're old creases . . . They'll be hard to get out.

DOCTOR: It's not important, Marchesa. The illusion is perfect. *(Then drawing closer and inviting her to take a position a bit farther forward of her daughter without totally blocking her.)* With your permission. That's right, take your position, there, slightly distant from her . . . a bit farther up now . . .

BELCREDI: To give the sense of time . . . of time's passage . . .

LADY MATILDA: *(Turning a bit in his direction.)* Twenty years later! What a disaster!

BELCREDI: Now, now, let's not exaggerate!

DOCTOR: *(Embarrassed, trying to remedy the situation.)* No, no! What I meant was . . . was the dress . . . to see it better . . .

BELCREDI: *(Laughing.)* Yes, well, as for the dress, Doctor, it's not a question of twenty years, but of eight hundred! An abyss! Do you really want to shove him into such a leap? *(Pointing first to FRIDA, then to the MARCHESA.)* From here to there? You'll be picking up the pieces after him. Think about it, my friends. Let's be serious. For us it's a mere twenty years, two dresses, and a masquerade. But for him, as you've said yourself, Doctor, if he has fixed himself in time, if he is living in that time with her *(Pointing at FRIDA.)*, eight hundred years ago, then the leap you are suggesting, the giddiness from that leap, will be such that when he suddenly drops down here among us . . . *(The DOCTOR signs negatively with his finger.)* You think not?

DOCTOR: No. Because life, my dear Baron, goes on. This life of ours—right here—will immediately become real for him as well. It will at once take hold of him, tear away the illusion, and reveal to him that the eight hundred years you speak of are no more than twenty. It's a trick, you see—a sort of trick—like the one in the Masonic rite—of jumping into the empty space which appears to be God knows how far, but is only a single step.

BELCREDI: Ah, what a discovery! Yes, of course! But just look at them there, Doctor, Frida and the Marchesa! Which is further advanced? The young think they are, but they're wrong. We're further advanced, we old people, Doctor, because time belongs more to us than to them.

DOCTOR: If only the past didn't alienate us so from each other.

BELCREDI: But it's not true! It doesn't! If those two there *(Indicating FRIDA and DI NOLLI.)* have to go through what we already have—grow old making more or less the same silly mistakes that we made, Doctor . . . well, you see, the illusion is that we enter life ahead of those who entered in front of us! But it's not true! We're no sooner born than we begin to die. So the one born first is further advanced than the one who was born later. And the youngest of us all is our father Adam. Look there! *(Pointing at FRIDA.)* The Marchesa Matilda of Tuscany! Eight hundred years younger than any of us! *(And he bows deeply to her.)*

DI NOLLI: Tito, Tito, please, no more joking.

BELCREDI: Ah, so you think I'm joking!

DI NOLLI: Yes, ever since we arrived . . .

BELCREDI: But I don't understand! I even dressed up as a Benedictine . . .

DI NOLLI: Yes, and for a very serious purpose . . .

BELCREDI: Serious, yes, for the others. For Frida, for example . . . *(Turning to the DOCTOR.)* I must confess, Doctor, I still have no idea what you want to do.

DOCTOR: *(Annoyed.)* You'll see! Just leave it to me, if you don't mind! At present you see the Marchesa dressed as she is . . .

BELCREDI: In other words, she also has to . . .

DOCTOR: Well, of course! Yes! We have a dress out there exactly like that one. When he takes it into his head that he's in the presence of the Marchesa Matilda of Canossa . . .

FRIDA: *(While speaking softly to DI NOLLI, she notices the DOCTOR's error.)* Tuscany! Tuscany!

DOCTOR: *(Annoyed.)* It's all the same!

BELCREDI: Ah, now I understand! He'll find the two of them standing there!

DOCTOR: Two of them! Exactly! And then . . .

FRIDA: *(Calling him to one side.)* Doctor. Please. May I have a moment?

DOCTOR: Here I am. *(Approaching to two young people, he pretends to give them an explanation.)*

BELCREDI: *(Quietly to LADY MATILDA.)* Good Heavens! In that case . . .

LADY MATILDA: *(Turning and looking him squarely in the face.)* What's the matter now?

BELCREDI: Are you really all this interested? To involve yourself like this? It's a huge task for a woman!

LADY MATILDA: For an ordinary woman, yes!

BELCREDI: No, not at all, my dear! For *any* woman! It's an enormous sacrifice . . .

LADY MATILDA: I owe it to him.

BELCREDI: You're lying! You know you'll come out of this smelling like a lily.

LADY MATILDA: Then where's the sacrifice?

BELCREDI: There's just enough not to disgrace you in others' eyes, but quite enough to offend me.

LADY MATILDA: And who cares a fig about you right now?

DI NOLLI: *(Coming closer.)* All right, it's time, I think we ought to get started . . . *(Turning to BERTHOLD.)* You! Go and call one of the other three!

BERTHOLD: At once, Signore. *(Goes out through the main door.)*

LADY MATILDA: First we have to pretend we're leaving.

DI NOLLI: Precisely. I've just called someone to see to your departure. *(To BELCREDI.)* You needn't bother. Better you stay here.

BELCREDI: *(Nodding ironically.)* Oh, I don't mind at all! Don't mind at all . . .

DI NOLLI: We mustn't make him suspicious again, you understand.

BELCREDI: Of course. I'm a negligible quantity!

DOCTOR: He must be made absolutely certain that we've left.

(LANDOLPH enters through the right exit followed by BERTHOLD.)

LANDOLPH: With your permission.

DI NOLLI: Of course, yes, come in, come in! Your name is Lolo, if I'm not mistaken.

LANDOLPH: Lolo or Landolph, whichever you prefer.

DI NOLLI: All right. Listen, now. The Doctor and the Marchesa will be leaving . . .

LANDOLPH: Very well. All that needs saying is that the pPontiff has conceded to receive him. He's in his rooms now, moaning and repentant for all the things he said, desperate that the pontiff will withhold his pardon. I trust you won't mind . . . but may I ask you to put on the robes again?

DOCTOR: Yes, yes, let's go, let's go . . .

LANDOLPH: Just a moment. May I suggest something? I suggest you add that the Marchesa Matilda of Tuscany also implored the pontiff for the grace to receive him.

LADY MATILDA: You see! He did recognize me!

LANDOLPH: No. I'm sorry. It means only that he has this great aversion toward the Marchesa who hosted the pope in her castle. It's strange— but history, as far as I know—but, then, you ladies and gentlemen are unquestionably in a position to know more than I—well, history nowhere says that Henry IV harbored a secret love for the Marchesa of Tuscany.

LADY MATILDA: *(Immediately.)* Not at all, no, certainly not! It's quite the opposite!

LANDOLPH: You see! That's what I thought! And yet he's always saying he loved her . . . And now he's afraid that her contempt for this secret love will work against him where the pontiff is concerned.

BELCREDI: Then it's your duty to make him understand that this aversion no longer exists.

LANDOLPH: Good. Very well.

LADY MATILDA: *(To LANDOLPH.)* Very well, indeed! *(Then to BELCREDI.)* In case you don't know, history has it that the pope yielded only because of the supplications of the Marchesa and the Abbot of Cluny. And may I add, my dear Belcredi—back in the time of our cavalcade, I was dead set on using that fact to impress on him that my heart was nowhere near as hostile to him as he might have imagined.

BELCREDI: What a surprise, my dear Marchesa! But do . . . do go on with your story . . .

LANDOLPH: In that case, madam could spare herself a double disguise and be presented with the Monsignore *(Indicating the DOCTOR.)* as the Marchesa of Tuscany.

DOCTOR: *(Quickly, forcefully.)* No, no! Any way but that! It would ruin everything! The confrontation must be sudden—must come as a shock.

No, Marchesa, no, let's go, let's go. When you return, it will be as the Duchess Adelaide, mother of the Empress. And then we'll leave. This is vital. He must know without a doubt that we have left. All right, now, come. Let's waste no more time. There's so much still to do.

(The DOCTOR, LADY MATILDA, and LANDOLPH exit right.)

FRIDA: I'm beginning to feel frightened again . . .

DI NOLLI: Not again, Frida!

FRIDA: It would be better if I'd seen him before . . .

DI NOLLI: There's nothing to be frightened of. Believe me.

FRIDA: You're certain he's not violent?

DI NOLLI: Of course not. He's calm.

BELCREDI: *(With ironic and sentimental affectation.)* Melancholy! Didn't you hear? He's in love with you.

FRIDA: *(Ironically.)* Oh, thanks a lot! That really helps!

BELCREDI: Why would he want to hurt you . . .

DI NOLLI: It will only take a moment . . .

FRIDA: Yes, but . . . there in the dark . . . with him . . .

DI NOLLI: Just one short moment. I'll be nearby, and the others just behind the door, ready to rush in. All he has to do is see your mother there in front of him and your part will be over . . .

BELCREDI: My fear, I'm afraid, is of another sort. Namely, that we're spinning our wheels!

DI NOLLI: Don't start in on that again. The remedy seems sound enough to me.

FRIDA: Yes, to me, too, I agree. It excites me terribly . . . I'm trembling.

BELCREDI: But the insane, my dears—though they aren't aware of it—have a certain felicity about them which we don't take into account . . .

DI NOLLI: *(Interrupting, annoyed.)* And what "felicity" would that be, I wonder? For God's sake!

BELCREDI: *(With force.)* The inability to reason!

DI NOLLI: And what has reason to do with it?

BELCREDI: Well, I dare say, as we've set it up, he'll need to do a bit of reasoning when he sees Frida and her mother. We're the ones who thought this up, remember.

DI NOLLI: Reasoning! Nonsense! We present him a double image of his own fantasy, as the Doctor has said!

BELCREDI: *(With a sudden outburst.)* God! I've never understood why those people take degrees in medicine!

DI NOLLI: *(Stunned.)* Who?

BELCREDI: Psychiatrists!

DI NOLLI: Oh, marvelous! Then what *should* they take degrees in?

FRIDA: If they're going to be psychiatrists!

BELCREDI: In law, dear hearts, in law! It's all just a lot of jabber! And the more they run on, the better they're taken to be! "Analogical elasticity!" "Sense of time passing!" And they're the first to announce that they can't perform miracles—when a miracle is precisely what's called for! But they know very well that when they confess they're not miracle-workers, the more impressed you will be by their seriousness. No, they don't perform miracles, but it's amazing how they always manage to land on their feet!

BERTHOLD: *(Who has been looking through the keyhole of the door at the right.)* There they are! There they are! They're coming in here!

DI NOLLI: In here?

BERTHOLD: It looks like he's coming, too! Yes, yes, he's coming, too! He's here!

DI NOLLI: All right, then, let's go! We're leaving! Hurry! *(Turning to BERTHOLD before leaving.)* You stay here!

BERTHOLD: Do I have to?

(Without answering, DI NOLLI, FRIDA, and BELCREDI hurry out the main door, leaving BERTHOLD in anxious bewilderment. The door at the right opens and LANDOLPH is the first to enter and bow. LADY MATILDA enters next wearing a mantle and a ducal crown, as in the first act, then the DOCTOR dressed as the Abbot of Cluny, and between them HENRY IV in regal dress. ORDULPH and HAROLD enter last.)

HENRY IV: *(Continuing a conversation presumably begun in the throne room.)* So then, tell me, how can I be so cunning if you believe me to be so obstinate . . .

DOCTOR: No, no, certainly not obstinate! Good Heavens!

HENRY IV: *(Smiling, pleased.)* Then you find me truly cunning?

DOCTOR: No, no, neither obstinate nor cunning!

HENRY IV: *(Stops and exclaims in a gently ironic tone that indicates that things cannot remain as they are.)* Monsignore . . . if obstinacy is not a vice that goes well with cunning, I at least hoped that, since you deny me the one, you would concede me a little of the other. I assure you, I have great need of it. But if it's your wish to keep it all for yourself . . .

DOCTOR: Ah, what's that, I? You find me cunning?

HENRY IV: No, Monsignore! How can you say that? I don't find you that in the least! *(Cutting himself short to turn to LADY MATILDA.)* Excuse me, a word in confidence with the Duchess. *(Leading her aside a few steps, he asks her earnestly and very secretly.)* Do you truly love your daughter?

LADY MATILDA: *(Bewildered.)* Well, of course . . . certainly . . .

HENRY IV: And would you have me compensate her with all of my love, all of my devotion for the grievous wrongs I have done her? And yet you must not believe all the dissoluteness that my enemies accuse me of.

LADY MATILDA: Oh, no. No, I never believed it . . .

HENRY IV: Well, then, is that what you want?

LADY MATILDA: What?

HENRY IV: That I return to loving your daughter. *(He looks at her and adds quickly in a mysterious tone of warning mixed with fear.)* Do not be a friend, do not be a friend of the Marchesa of Tuscany!

LADY MATILDA: I must remind you that she has not begged, has not pleaded for your pardon any less than we.

HENRY IV: *(Quickly, softly, trembling.)* Don't tell me! Don't tell me! Can't you see how it affects me?

LADY MATILDA: *(Looks at him, then very softly, as if in confidence.)* Are you still in love with her?

HENRY IV: *(Bewildered.)* Still? How can you say that—still? How can you know? No one knows! No one must!

LADY MATILDA: Perhaps she knows, then, yes, perhaps, if she has begged so hard for you!

HENRY IV: *(Looks at her for a while, then speaks.)* So, you love your daughter, you say? *(Brief pause, then turns to the DOCTOR with a hint of laughter.)* Ah, Monsignore, it's true. I only discovered I had a wife afterwards. And that was . . . late in the day. Too late. But, yes, even now, even now I have her, there can be no doubt I have her, but I swear to you that I hardly ever give her a thought. It may be a sin, but I really have no feeling for her—she has no place in my heart. But what is most amazing of all is that her mother has no place for her in her heart either! Admit it, my lady, you feel very little for her! *(Turning to the DOCTOR in exasperation.)* All she talks to me about is the other woman! *(Growing more and more excited.)* She insists! A kind of insistence I simply don't understand!

LANDOLPH: *(Humbly.)* It's possible, Majesty, that she's trying to change your opinion of the Marchesa of Tuscany. *(Disturbed at having permitted himself to make the observation, he adds quickly.)* What I mean, of course, is at this moment . . .

HENRY IV: Do you, too, now maintain that she was friendly to me?

LANDOLPH: Yes, at this moment, yes, Majesty!

LADY MATILDA: There you are, yes, for precisely this reason . . .

HENRY IV: I understand. You're saying that you don't believe I love her. I understand. I understand. No one has ever believed it. No one has even suspected. So much the better. Basta. Now an end. *(Stopping short, he turns to the DOCTOR with an altered mind and face.)* Did you notice, Monsignore? The conditions the pope gives for revoking my excommunication have nothing, nothing, to do with his reason for excommunicating me in the first place. Tell Pope Gregory that we will meet again at Bressanone. And you, my lady, if you should happen to meet your daughter in the courtyard of your friend the Marchesa's castle . . . ah, what can I tell you? Have her come up. We'll see whether I succeed in keeping her here as both wife and Empress. Many women have come here and presented themselves, assuring and reassuring me that they were she—the wife that I knew I had . . . and, yes, sometimes I even tried to . . . well, nothing to be ashamed of there—she was, after all, my wife!—But when they said that they were Bertha, that they were from Susa—all of them—and I don't know why—each one—began to laugh! *(As if confidentially.)* Do you understand? We were in bed—I was naked—and, well, so was she—and why not, for God's sake—absolutely naked—a man and a woman . . . it's only natural . . . It's times like that we forget who we are . . . our clothes hanging there . . . like ghosts! *(In another tone of voice, in confidence to the DOCTOR.)* And I think, Monsignore, that ghosts, in general, are no more than trivial disorders of the spirit—images we're unable to contain within the bounds of sleep. They also reveal themselves in waking hours, during the day, and they frighten us. I'm always terrified when at night I see them hovering in front of me—all those disordered images—like laughing horsemen that have jumped from their mounts. Sometimes I'm even frightened by the pulsing of the blood in my veins in the silence of the night—like the thud of footsteps in distant rooms . . . But enough of this. I've kept you standing here far too long. My lady! Monsignore! *(He accompanies them to the main door, where he dismisses them, accepting their bows. LADY MATILDA and the DOCTOR leave. He closes the door and suddenly turns around, changed.)* Clowns! Buffoons! Idiots! Like playing a color-organ! All I did was touch it and: white, red, yellow, green! And that other one there! Peter Damiani! Ha! Ha! Perfect! I guessed him right! He won't be showing his face around here again! *(As all this gushes out of him in a joyous but frenzied torrent, he moves about excitedly from one place to another, shifting his eyes this way and that till finally he catches sight of BERTHOLD, who by this time is more than dumbfounded and terrified by the unexpected change. He stops in front of him and points him out to the other three companions who are equally bewildered by amazement.)* Look at him here, this imbecile, watching me with his mouth agape . . . *(Taking him by the shoulders and shaking him.)* Don't you understand? Don't you see how I force them to deck themselves out, how I treat them like the shit they are, how I make them prance around in front of me like frightened clowns! And only one thing terrifies them—oh!—that I'll rip off their clownish masks and reveal their disguise—as if I wasn't the one who forced them into it in the first place to satisfy my own pleasure of playing the madman!

LANDOLPH, HAROLD, ORDULPH: *(Upset, amazed, looking at each other.)* What? What did he say? But then . . . this means . . .

HENRY IV: *(Turning suddenly at their exclamations, and shouting imperiously.)* Enough! End it! I'm fed up! *(Then suddenly, as if, after thinking it over, he is incapable of coming to terms with it and isn't able to believe it.)* Damn their impudence! Damn their showing themselves to me, here, now, and with her lover tagging along behind, pretending—the nerve of it!—pretending they're doing it out of pity! Mustn't upset the poor bastard! He's already at the end of his rope! Running out of time, out of world, out of life! Otherwise the poor wretch would never submit to such tyranny! Every day, every moment, they expect others to be what *they* want them to be! But that's not oppression! Oh, no! It's how they think, how they see, how they feel! To each his own! And you have your way, too! Even you! But what would yours be like, I wonder? To be like sheep? Miserable, unsteady, uncertain? And they take advantage of you like this, put you down, make you do what *they* want, so that you'll see and feel as *they* do! At least it's what they think. It's part of their illusion. Because what have they really succeeded in imposing on you? Words! Words that everyone can interpret and repeat in any way he wants! Yes, and that's exactly how what is known as public opinion is formed. And God help the man who one fine day discovers himself labeled with one of these words that everyone repeats! Madman, for example! Or . . . oh, what would another be? Imbecile! Tell me, how would you like it if you learned that someone is going around persuading others that you are exactly as *he* sees you to be—doing everything possible to classify you in other people's estimation according to his *own* personal judgment of you? Mad! Mad! I'm not saying this to be a joke. Earlier, before I fell from my horse and hit my head . . . *(He stops short as he notices the other four men's agitation as they grow more nervous and bewildered than before.)* Why are you looking at each other like that? *(He imitates their amazement grotesquely.)* Ah! Eh! What a revelation! Am I or am I not? Oh, go on, say it, yes, I *am* mad! *(He becomes terrifying.)* All right, by God, down on your knees! Down on your knees! *(He forces them down to their knees, one after the other.)* I order you to kneel down in front of me and touch the floor with your forehead three times! Down! Everyone must assume this position before madmen! *(As he sees the four men on their knees in front of him, he senses his ferocious joy fading and becomes contemptuous.)* On your feet, sheep! You obeyed me! Why? You could have forced me into a straightjacket. Crush a man with the weight of a single word? It's nothing! Like swatting a fly! A man's life can be crushed by the weight of a word. That includes all of us. The weight of the dead. Here I am. Here. Can you seriously believe that Henry IV is still alive? Yet here I am, talking and ordering you around, you who are alive! And it's the way I want you! Do you see that to be a joke as well? That the dead continue to live their lives? Oh, yes, it's a joke in here, all right . . . but once you leave here and enter the living world . . . Day is breaking. All time is before you. The dawn! This day lies spread out before us, you say—let's make of it what we will! But will you? Will you say good-bye to traditions? Good-bye to worn-out customs? And when you speak? Will you use only words that have not been repeated from the beginning of time? No! And you will think that you are alive and living! But you will only be remasticating the life of the dead! *(He stops in front of BERTHOLD who by now is stupefied.)* You don't understand a thing, do you?—What's your name?

BERTHOLD: Me? Oh . . . Berthold . . .

HENRY IV: Idiot! What do you mean—Berthold! Just between the two of us, I'm asking, what's your name?

BERTHOLD: My . . . my na . . . name . . . is really . . . Fino . . .

HENRY IV: *(Feeling the sense of warning and admonition from the others, he immediately turns to silence them.)* Fino?

BERTHOLD: Fino Pagliuca, sir.

HENRY IV: *(Turning again to the others.)* Yes, I've heard you talking together many times, using your names.—*(To LANDOLPH.)* Your name is Lolo?

LANDOLPH: Yes, Signore . . . *(Then in a burst of joy.)* My God! But then . . .

HENRY IV: *(Without pause, brusquely.)* What?

LANDOLPH: *(Quickly, turning pale.)* No . . . I mean . . .

HENRY IV: That I'm not mad? No, of course not! Can't you see? It's all a joke on those who think I am. *(To HAROLD.)* Your name is Franco. *(To ORDULPH.)* And you . . . wait, let's see . . .

ORDULPH: Momo!

HENRY IV: Yes, Momo! Nice, isn't it?

LANDOLPH: But, then . . . oh, God . . .

HENRY IV: What? Nothing! Let's just have a good, long laugh over it! *(And he laughs.)* Ha-ha-ha-ha-ha-ha!

LANDOLPH, HAROLD, ORDULPH: *(Looking at each other, uncertain, bewildered, between joy and alarm.)* He's cured? Is it true? But how?

HENRY IV: Quiet! Quiet! *(To BERTHOLD.)* You're not laughing? Are you still offended? Don't be. My words weren't aimed at you. It's convenient for everyone, you see. Convenient to believe that certain people are mad, because then they have an excuse to lock them up. And do you know why? Because they can't endure to hear what they have to say. What can I say about those people who just left? That one's a whore, the other a filthy libertine, and the third an impostor . . . "No, no, it's not true," everyone would cry. No one would believe it! But they all stand there, terrified, listening to me. But why, I'd like to know, why, if what I say isn't true? Who could possibly believe the words of a madman! But does that stop them listening to me with eyes wide open with fright? Why? Tell me. You tell me. Why? I'm calm now, don't you see?

BERTHOLD: Well, maybe . . . maybe they think that . . .

HENRY IV: No, my dear boy . . . no . . . Look me straight in the eyes. I'm not saying it's true—don't be frightened. Nothing is true. Just look into my eyes.

BERTHOLD: All right . . . there . . . now what?

HENRY IV: You see? Do you see it? You, too! You have it too now . . . there's fear in your eyes! Because at this moment I appear mad to you!—There's the proof! There's the proof for you! *(And he laughs.)*

LANDOLPH: *(Gathering his courage, speaking for the others, exasperated.)* What proof?

HENRY IV: Your fright, because now, at this very moment, I again appear to you to be mad! And, by God, you know it! You believed me! You believed all along that I was mad! Didn't you? *(He looks at them for a while, seeing their terror.)* You see? This fear of yours? You feel it can suddenly turn into terror—rip the ground from under you, swallow up the air you breathe. It can't be otherwise, gentlemen. Do you know what it means to stand in front of a madman? To be face-to-face with someone who shakes the very foundation of everything you've built up in and around you? That logic, the logic of all your constructions? But what can you expect? The insane, bless them, construct without logic! Or, better yet, with a logic light as a feather! Always changing, never the same! This way today, that way tomorrow! Who knows! You stand fast and they float! Never the same! Never the same! You say: "But it can't be!" For them everything can be! You say: "But it's not true!" But *why* isn't it true? Because it doesn't seem true to you—and you—and you—*(Points to each of them.)* and to a hundred thousand others like you. But then we'd have to take a look at what *does* seem true to these hundred thousand others who are not considered to be mad. Ah, and what a marvelous spectacle they make of it, my friends, with their common agreement, the flowers of their logic! When I was a child I believed that the reflection of the moon in a puddle was real. So many things seemed real! I believed what they told me, those other people, and I was happy! You must hold with all your might to what seems true to you today, and with all your might to what will seem true to you tomorrow, even if it's the opposite of what you thought was true yesterday! God have mercy on you if you are ever caught, as I am, by an idea that you can never escape from, that can truly drive you mad. Imagine yourself beside someone, looking into his eyes, as one day I looked into someone's eyes—and you'll know what it's like being a beggar in front of a door that you know you will never enter. The one who enters will never be you, but someone else, someone who sees the world differently, who touches it differently, someone you don't even know, someone who sees and touches you out of his own impenetrable world . . . *(A long pause. The shadows in the room begin to darken, causing the intensification of that sense of bewilderment and profound consternation shared by the four masqueraders. The Great Masquerader remains aloof and absorbed in the thought of the terrible misery that is not his alone, but that of all humanity. Then, pulling himself together, and not sensing the presence of the four men around him, looks around for them and speaks.)* It has grown dark in here.

ORDULPH: *(Quickly, coming forward.)* Shall I go for a lamp?

HENRY IV: *(Ironically.)* The lamp, yes . . . You think I don't know that as soon as I turn my back and go off to bed with my oil lamp, you turn on all the electric lights in here as well as in the throne room? I pretend not to notice . . .

ORDULPH: Ah! Well, then . . .

HENRY IV: No, it would blind me.—I want my own lamp.

ORDULPH: Right. It's all ready for you, just behind the door. *(He leaves through the main door, returning immediately with an ancient lamp that is held by a ring at the top.)*

HENRY IV: *(Takes the lamp and points to the table in the gallery.)* Ah! There we are! A little light! Sit down . . . there, around the table. Oh, but not like that! Relax . . . not so stiff. *(To HAROLD.)* There, now, like that . . . *(He poses him, then to BERTHOLD.)* And you like this . . . *(Poses him.)* There, that's right . . . *(He sits down as well.)* And I'll sit here . . . *(Turning his head in the direction of a window.)* Too bad we can't just order a nice little moonbeam . . . She's very good to us, the moon . . . very useful . . . especially to me . . . I often have a great need of her here inside me, and lose myself in her gaze from my window. Who would guess, to look at her up there, that she knows eight hundred years have passed, and that I can't possibly be Henry IV gazing up at her from my window like any poor ordinary man? But look, look, what a magnificent night scene we have here: The Emperor surrounded by his faithful counselors . . . How do you like it?

LANDOLPH: *(Softly to HAROLD, not wishing to break the spell.)* And to think it wasn't true!

HENRY IV: True? What's that?

LANDOLPH: *(Hesitating, as if to excuse himself.)* No . . . well . . . I mean, as I was saying to him . . . to Berthold here . . . he only began working here today . . . well, I was saying this morning what a pity to be dressed like this, and with so many other splendid costumes in the wardrobe, and with a room like . . . like that one . . . *(Points in the direction of the throne room.)*

HENRY IV: Pity? What's a pity?

LANDOLPH: Well . . . I mean, that we didn't know . . .

HENRY IV: That this comedy here was being played for fun?

LANDOLPH: Well, because we thought . . .

HAROLD: *(Coming to his aid.)* That it was all to be taken very seriously!

HENRY IV: What do you mean? Doesn't it seem serious to you?

LANDOLPH: Yes, but if you say that . . .

HENRY IV: What I say is that you are a pack of fools! You should have known how to act out the fantasy for yourselves! Not for me, not for those who visit me from time to time, but like this, like this, the way you are now, naturally, day after day—*(To BERTHOLD, taking him by the arm.)* for *yourselves!* You could have eaten, slept, even scratched an itch if you felt the urge, feeling alive, truly alive, *in this fiction,* living in the history of the eleven-hundreds, here, in the court of your Emperor Henry IV! You could have told yourselves from this remote period of time, long buried in the past, so colorful, so sepulchral, eight centuries back, that men of the twentieth century are tormenting themselves in a state of terrible confusion, grappling with endless anxiety to know what fortune, what fate, that holds them in such anguish, such agitation, has in store for them. But no! You're already a part of history! With me! However sad my lot may be, however dreadful the facts and bitter the battles I have fought, however sorrowful the events—it is all already history, and none of it, none of it, can ever, ever, be changed! Do you understand? Fixed in time! Forever!—As for you, you may sit there in peace and comfort, awed by how every effect follows obediently from its cause, with perfect logic, how every event unfolds precisely and coherently in its every detail. The pleasure . . . the pleasure of history . . . how grand it is!

LANDOLPH: Beautiful, beautiful!

HENRY IV: Beautiful, yes, but finished. Now that you know, I simply can't do it anymore. *(Picks up the lamp, about to go off to bed.)* Nor could any of you, if up till now you haven't understood the reason for it. I'm sick of it! *(Almost to himself, with violent but controlled anger.)* By God, I'll make her regret she ever came here! Dressing up as my mother-in-law! And he as an abbot! And a doctor with them, to study me! Who knows, maybe even hoping to cure me! Clowns! I must, at least, have the pleasure of slapping one of them in the face! Yes, him, he's the one. A famous swordsman, they say. He'll run me through . . . We'll see, we'll see . . . *(A knock at the main door.)* Who is it?

GIOVANNI: *(From off.)* Deo gratias!

HAROLD: *(Happily, at the thought of playing another joke.)* Ah, it's Giovanni, Giovanni, coming to play the monk tonight, as usual . . .

ORDULPH: *(Rubbing his hands together in anticipation.)* Oh, yes, yes, let's let him do it!

HENRY IV: *(Suddenly, severe.)* You fool! You'd play a joke on a poor old man who does it only out of love for me? Why?

LANDOLPH: *(To ORDULPH.)* It's got to look like the truth, you understand?

HENRY IV: Ah! Exactly! Yes! Like the truth! It's the only way truth can never be a joke! *(He goes to open the door to admit GIOVANNI dressed as a humble monk with a roll of parchment under his arm.)* Come in, Father, come in! *(Assuming a tone of tragic gravity and gloomy resentment.)* All the documents of my life and reign that are favorable to me have been destroyed, deliberately, by my enemies. The only thing to have escaped destruction is this account of my life, written by a humble monk who is devoted to me—and you want to laugh at it? *(He turns affectionately to GIOVANNI and invites him to sit at the table.)* Here, Father, sit here, sit here. And here's the lamp. *(Places the lamp he is still holding on the table near GIO-VANNI.)* Write, write.

GIOVANNI: *(Unrolls the parchment and prepares to take dictation.)* I'm ready, Majesty!

HENRY IV: *(Dictating.)* "The declaration of peace proclaimed at Mainz benefited the poor and the good as much as it harmed the bad and the powerful." *(The curtain begins to fall.)* "It brought wealth to the former, hunger and misery to the latter . . .

END OF ACT II

ACT THREE

The throne room. Dark. The back wall is scarcely visible. The canvases of the two portraits have been removed from their frames and standing in the niches behind the frames are FRIDA, dressed as the Marchesa of Tuscany, and CARLO DI NOLLI as Henry IV. As the curtain rises, the stage is empty for a moment. The door at the left opens and HENRY IV enters carrying the lamp by the ring at the top. Turning, he calls to the FOUR YOUNG MEN and GIOVANNI who supposedly are in the adjoining room into which he speaks, as at the close of the second act.

HENRY IV: No. Stay where you are. I can manage. Good night. *(He closes the door and moves, sad and exhausted, across the room toward the second exit on the right that leads to his apartments.)*

FRIDA: *(As soon as she sees that he has gone a little past the throne, she whispers from her niche like one about to faint from fright.)* Henry . . .

HENRY IV: *(Stopping at the sound of her voice, as if stabbed traitorously in the back, he turns a terror-stricken face to the back wall and instinctively raises his arm in self-defense.)* Who's there? *(It is not really a question, but an exclamation tremulous with terror that expects no reply from the darkness and the dreadful silence of the hall that suddenly fills him with the suspicion that perhaps he is indeed mad.)*

FRIDA: *(At his terrified exclamation, and no less terrified by the rôle she has agreed to play, repeats a bit louder.)* Henry . . . *(Although she has tried to play her assigned rôle, she nonetheless stretches her neck out a bit beyond the frame to make certain DI NOLLI is still in his niche. HENRY IV utters a cry and lets the lamp fall in order to wrap his arms around his head and try to flee. FRIDA jumps from the niche onto the ledge, shouting like a woman demented,)* Henry! Henry! Oh, I'm so frightened! So frightened!

(At this, DI NOLLI also leaps onto the ledge and then to the floor and runs to FRIDA who continues her uncontrollable screaming and is on the verge of fainting. The door at the left bursts open and all the others rush into the room: the DOCTOR, LADY MATILDA, also dressed as the Marchesa of Tuscany, TITO BELCREDI, LANDOLPH, HAROLD, ORDULPH, BERTHOLD, GIOVANNI. One of them suddenly turns on the light: a strange glow is given off by lightbulbs hidden in the ceiling in such a way that only the upper half of the set is illuminated. Though jolted by the terrifying moment that still causes his entire body to tremble, HENRY IV stands watching, stunned by the unexpected invasion of people. Paying him no

attention, everyone rushes in concern to offer comfort and assistance to the still shaking FRIDA who is moaning and raving in DI NOLLI's arms. Everyone is speaking in a mass of confusion.)

DI NOLLI: No, no, Frida . . . I'm here . . . I'm with you!

DOCTOR: *(Coming with the others.)* That's it! It's over! He's cured!

LADY MATILDA: He's cured, Frida! Look! You see? He's cured!

DI NOLLI: *(Astonished.)* Cured?

BELCREDI: It was all a joke! Calm down!

FRIDA: No! I'm afraid! I'm afraid!

LADY MATILDA: Of what? Look at him! It wasn't true! It's not true!

DI NOLLI: *(Astonished.)* Not true? What are you saying? He's cured?

DOCTOR: It would appear so! As far as I'm concerned . . .

BELCREDI: Oh, it *is,* it *is!* They told us so! *(Indicates the FOUR YOUNG MEN.)*

LADY MATILDA: Yes, for a long time! He confided in them!

DI NOLLI: *(Now more indignant than astonished.)* But how? If until only a short while ago . . . ?

BELCREDI: Hmm! It was an act! He was having a good laugh at our expense! While we in good faith . . .

DI NOLLI: But it's not possible! Deceiving even his sister, right up to her death . . . ?

(HENRY IV has remained apart, looking at one and then another as they rain down abuse and derision on him for the now-revealed cruel joke they take it all to be. The gleam in his eye indicates that he is contemplating a revenge that his violent contempt will not yet permit to take definitive shape. Deeply offended, and with the clear idea of taking as true the fiction they have insidiously worked up, he jumps up, shouting at his nephew.)

HENRY IV: Go on! Go on talking!

DI NOLLI: *(Startled by the shout.)* Go on what?

HENRY IV: *Your* sister isn't the only one who's dead!

DI NOLLI: *(Startled.)* My sister? No, *yours!* You forced her till the end to appear before you here as your mother Agnes!

HENRY IV: And you're saying she wasn't your mother?

DI NOLLI: *My* mother, yes, exactly!

HENRY IV: Your mother is dead for me, old and far away! But you have just newly descended from your niche, and what do *you* know, how do you *know* whether I haven't wept for her, secretly, for a long, long time? Even dressed as I am!

LADY MATILDA: *(In consternation, looking at the others.)* What is he saying?

DOCTOR: *(Greatly impressed, observing him.)* Shh, not so loud, for heaven's sake . . .

HENRY IV: What am I saying? I'm asking all of you if Agnes was not the mother of Henry IV! *(He turns to FRIDA as if she really were the Marchesa of Tuscany.)* You, Marchesa, ought surely to know! Or so it would seem!

FRIDA: *(Still frightened, draws closer to DI NOLLI.)* No, I don't, I don't!

DOCTOR: There, you see, the delirium is returning . . . Everyone quiet now!

BELCREDI: *(Indignant.)* And what delirium would that be, Doctor? He's back to acting his rôle!

HENRY IV: *(Suddenly.)* Am I? And yet it's you who have just emptied those two niches, and *he* stands before me here as Henry IV . . .

BELCREDI: I think we've had enough of this joke!

HENRY IV: Joke?

DOCTOR: *(To BELCREDI, loudly.)* Don't provoke him, for God's sake!

BELCREDI: *(Ignoring him, even louder.)* They said so! They! *(Indicates the FOUR MEN.)* Right over there!

HENRY IV: *(Turning to look at them.)* You? Called it a joke?

LANDOLPH: *(Timid, embarrassed.)* No . . . no, no, really . . . we said you were cured!

BELCREDI: Can we *end* this once and for all! Doesn't it appear to you, Marchesa, that the sight of you and him *(Indicating DI NOLLI.)* dressed as you are, is becoming an intolerable puerility?

LADY MATILDA: Oh, shut up, will you! Who cares *how* we're dressed if he's really cured?

HENRY IV: Cured? Yes! I *am* cured! *(To BELCREDI.)* Ah, but not to end all this quite as quickly as you may think! *(Attacking him.)* Are you aware that not for twenty years has anyone dared to appear before me as you and that gentleman there are dressed? *(Indicating the DOCTOR.)*

BELCREDI: Indeed I do! This morning, in fact, I appeared before you dressed as . . .

HENRY IV: As a monk! I know!

BELCREDI: And you took me for Peter Damiani! And I didn't even laugh, believing, in fact, that you were . . .

HENRY IV: Mad! Does it make you laugh now, seeing her dressed as she is, now that I'm cured? And yet you might have considered that to my eyes the way she looks now—*(Interrupting himself with a gesture of contempt.)* Ah! *(Quickly turning to the DOCTOR.)* Are you a doctor?

DOCTOR: I, yes . . .

HENRY IV: And it was your idea to dress her up as the Marchesa of Tuscany? Are you aware, Doctor, that you came very close to plunging my mind back into the dark abyss of madness? Why, we had living, breathing portraits that spoke, that jumped from their frames! *(He contemplates FRIDA and DI NOLLI, then looks at the MARCHESA, and finally at the costume he himself is wearing.)* Ah, a beautiful combination, Doctor . . . marvelous . . . two couples . . . perfect replicas . . . marvelous, marvelous: just the thing for a madman . . . *(A slight motion of the hand toward BEL-CREDI.)* It must seem to him a carnival celebration out of season, hmm? *(Turning to look at him.)* But now to get out of this masquerade *(Indicates his costume.)* so that I can come away with you. Isn't that so?

BELCREDI: With me? With us?

HENRY IV: Ah, but where to? The club? White tie and tails? Or home, both of us, with the Marchesa?

BELCREDI: Wherever you like! At any rate you can't want to stay on here alone now, continuing in this unfortunate carnival-day joke of yours, now would you? It's quite incredible how you managed to keep it up all these years, after you'd recovered!

HENRY IV: Yes, well, you must remember, Doctor . . . after I fell from my horse and cracked my head, I really was mad . . . for how long, I don't know . . .

DOCTOR: Ah, there you are! You see! For a long time?

HENRY IV: *(Very rapidly, to the DOCTOR.)* Yes, Doctor, I would say so, a long time . . . about twelve years. *(Quickly returning to BELCREDI.)* All of which means, my dear Belcredi, that from the moment of that cavalcade accident I was totally unaware of everything that happened in the world about me—to you, to me—how things changed, how friends betrayed me, how others stepped into my shoes . . . oh, let's say, took my place in the heart of the woman I loved! I didn't know who had died! I didn't know who had disappeared! And I can tell you this for certain, none of it was a joke to me—as it seems to have been for you!

BELCREDI: No, no, that's not what I meant. I'm sorry. I meant afterwards.

HENRY IV: Oh, did you? Afterwards? One day . . . *(He stops and turns to the DOCTOR.)* A most interesting case, Doctor! Study me, study me carefully! *(Trembling as he speaks.)* All by itself, I don't know how, but one day, the trouble here . . . *(Touches his forehead.)* the trouble here was . . . was gone. I open my eyes, little by little, not knowing am I awake or asleep. I know then . . . I'm awake. And I start touching, this, that . . . I see clearly again . . . And, yes, he's right, he's right . . . *(Indicating BELCREDI.)*

Off with these things, this masquerade, this nightmare! Open the windows! Let's breathe in life! Outside! Let's run! *(Suddenly calming his ardor.)* Where to? To do what? To have everyone secretly point to me and whisper: "Henry IV!" when I'm not like that anymore, but out there with you, arm in arm, my dear, dear friends!

BELCREDI: Of course not! Why are you saying that? Why?

LADY MATILDA: Who would do such a thing! It's not possible! It was an unfortunate accident!

HENRY IV: But they thought me mad even before it happened! *(To BELCREDI.)* Which you know very well! You led the crowd against anyone who tried to defend me!

BELCREDI: Oh, come now! It was all in fun!

HENRY IV: Have a look at my hair. See here? *(Shows him the hair on the nape of his neck.)*

BELCREDI: But mine is gray, too!

HENRY IV: Yes, with one difference! Mine went gray *here*, as Henry IV, and I didn't even know it. One morning I opened my eyes and I was shocked, shocked because I realized that not only my hair had gone gray, but everything, everything in me, that it was over, everything collapsed, fallen into ruin, gray through and through . . . I had arrived at a banquet hungry as a bear and it had already been cleared away.

BELCREDI: Yes, but surely the others couldn't have . . .

HENRY IV: *(Quickly.)* Couldn't have what? Waited till I was cured? Oh, certainly not. Not even those who rode behind me in the cavalcade and repeatedly pricked at my saddled horse till it bled . . .

DI NOLLI: *(Alarmed.)* What? What?

HENRY IV: Yes, treacherously, to make the horse rear back and me to fall!

LADY MATILDA: *(Quickly, horrified.)* This is the first I've heard of this!

HENRY IV: Was this also "all in fun"?

LADY MATILDA: But who? Who was behind us?

HENRY IV: Does it matter! All of them! All who went on with their feasting! All who would happily have left me their scraps of miserable pity! The paltry remnants of remorse! Thank you for nothing! *(Turning to the DOCTOR abruptly.)* Tell me, Doctor, this case of mine—it must be quite new in the annals of madness, don't you think? I preferred to remain mad because I found everything here to hand for this exquisite new fantasy! I chose to live out my madness totally aware of my action and in so doing take vengeance on the stone that played so brutally with my head! The squalid and empty solitude I saw, when I again opened my eyes, made me determined to deck it out with all the color and splendor of that distant carnival day when you . . . *(Looks at LADY MATILDA and points out FRIDA to her.)* Ah, there you are!—when you, Marchesa, had your triumph! I determined, by God, to obligate all who came into my presence to play out that carnival masquerade of long ago, that masquerade which—for you but not for me—was the joke of the day! I would manage it so that it would last forever—a joke no longer, not a chance—but reality, the reality of true madness! Here, this very place, everyone in costume, a throne room, and these four counselors of mine—privy, as we say—and, of course, as you all know, traitors! *(Turning abruptly toward them.)* I wonder what you thought you would gain by revealing that I was cured! If I am cured, your presence here is superfluous, and you have just been fired! Confiding in others is . . . well . . . truly the act of a madman! Ah, but now it's time for me to accuse *you!* *(Turning to the others.)* Do you know? They thought that they and I together would continue the joke by turning the tables—on you—and you not know a thing! *(He bursts out laughing. The others laugh, too, but disconcertedly, except for LADY MATILDA.)*

BELCREDI: *(To DI NOLLI.)* Ah! Did you hear that! Not bad!

DI NOLLI: *(To the FOUR YOUNG MEN.)* You?

HENRY IV: But we must forgive them. These . . . *(Indicating his own costume.)* these for me are the caricature of that other masquerade that goes on forever—every day, every minute—except with me it's an obvious choice—whereas you are clowns, however involuntary. *(Indicating BELCREDI.)* Without knowing it, you disguise yourselves as who you think you are. And so we must forgive these young men. They don't yet realize that the clothes they use to cover themselves are . . . who they are. *(Turning again to BELCREDI.)* You get used to it soon enough. How difficult can it be to walk around like a tragic character *(Imitates the walk of a tragic character.)* in a room like this? Listen to this, Doctor. I remember a priest—Irish to the core—handsome—who one November day sat dozing in the sun, his arm resting on the back of a park bench. Drowned in the golden delight of that sunny warmth, it must have seemed to him like summer. I can't help feeling that at that moment he was utterly unaware of being a priest. He was dreaming. Who knows of what! A little rascal of a boy passed by then, a flower in his hand that he'd torn up down to the roots, and tickled the priest, here, on the neck. I saw him open his eyes, eyes filled with laughter, smiling blissfully from the utter forgetfulness of his dream. Then suddenly he straightened up, collected himself in his priest's robes, and that same seriousness returned to his eyes as you have seen in mine, because Irish priests defend their Catholic faith with the same fervor that I use to defend the sacred rights of hereditary monarchy. I am cured, ladies and gentlemen, because I play the part of a madman like a past master—and I do it quietly! Your trouble is that you live in your madness with such a flurry of agitation that you neither know nor see it!

BELCREDI: The conclusion being, I suppose, that *we* are the mad ones!

HENRY IV: *(Containing an outburst.)* If you *weren't* mad, you, she— *(Indicating the Marchesa.)* both of you—would you have come here to see me?

BELCREDI: The fact is, I came here believing you *were* mad!

HENRY IV: *(Suddenly, very loud, indicating the MARCHESA.)* And she?

BELCREDI: Ah, well, that I don't know . . . I see her fascinated by everything you say . . . enchanted by this "conscious" madness of yours! *(Turning to her.)* Dressed as you are, Marchesa, you could just as easily stay behind and live out this madness on the spot . . .

MATILDA: You're very insolent!

HENRY IV: *(Quickly, placatingly.)* Don't listen to him. Ignore him. He insists on provoking me, against all the Doctor's orders. *(Turning to BEL-CREDI.)* Why in God's name should I trouble myself with what happened between us—the share you had with her in my misfortune— *(Indicates the MARCHESA and then turns to her and points at BEL-CREDI.)* or the part he now plays in your life! *This* is my life! *This!* And it's not *yours!* Not *your* life! *Your* life, the life you grew *old* in, is not the life *I* lived! *(To LADY MATILDA.)* Is this what you wanted? To tell me, to show me? This? This sacrifice of yours? Dressing up according to the Doctor's recommendation? Very good, Doctor! Very, very good! "As we were then, hm, and how we are now?" But I'm not mad as you understand madness, Doctor. I am fully aware that that man there *(Indicates DI NOLLI.)* cannot be me, because *I* am Henry IV, I, do you understand? I, here, Henry IV, for twenty years, fixed in this eternal masquerade! She's the one who lived those years—*(Indicates the MARCHESA.)* she's the one who enjoyed them—those twenty years—and become— look at her there—someone I no longer recognize. This is how I know her . . . how I recognize her . . . *(Indicates FRIDA and draws close to her.)* This is how I know her . . . this is the Marchesa . . . forever. *(To the others.)* You all seem to me like children I can easily frighten. *(To FRIDA.)* And you're frightened, too, child, by the joke they persuaded you to take part in, not knowing that for me it could never be the game they thought, but this terrible prodigy: The dream come alive in you—more than alive! There—in that frame—you were an image; but now they've made you flesh and blood. You're mine! You're mine! Mine! Mine by right! *(He wraps her in his arms, laughing like a madman, while all the others cry out in terror. As they approach to tear FRIDA from his arms, he becomes terrifying, shouts to his FOUR YOUNG MEN.)* Hold them! Hold onto them! I order you to hold them back!

(The FOUR YOUNG MEN, amazed, yet fascinated, move almost automatically to hold back DI NOLLI, the DOCTOR, and BELCREDI.)

BELCREDI: *(Quickly frees himself and hurls himself at HENRY IV.)* Let her go! Let her go! You're not mad!

HENRY IV: *(In a flash draws the sword from the side of LANDOLPH who is beside him.)* Not mad, am I? Take that! *(And he wounds him in the stomach. There is a cry of horror and the others rush to help BELCREDI who is in turmoil.)*

DI NOLLI: Did he wound you?

BERTHOLD: He's wounded! He's wounded!

DOCTOR: I warned you!

FRIDA: Oh, God!

DI NOLLI: Frida—come here!

LADY MATILDA: He's mad! Mad!

DI NOLLI: Hold him!

BELCREDI: *(Protesting furiously as they carry him out through the door at the left.)* No! You're *not* mad! He's *not* mad! He's *not* mad!

(They go off shouting through the left door and continue shouting well beyond the exit until suddenly there is an even more piercing shout from LADY MATILDA. Then silence)

HENRY IV: *(Has remained onstage surrounded by LANDOLPH, HAROLD, and ORDULPH, his eyes wide with terror at the life of his own fiction that in a single moment has forced him into this crime.)* Now . . . yes, now . . . I have no choice . . . *(He calls them around him as if to protect him.)* . . . here together . . . here . . . together . . . and forever!

END OF PLAY

A LIST FOR FURTHER READING

Bassanese, Fiora. *Understanding Luigi Pirandello.* Columbia, 1997.

Bentley, Eric. *The Pirandello Commentaries.* Evanston, 1986.

Bishop, Tom. *Pirandello and the French Theatre.* New York, 1960.

Büdel, Oscar. *Pirandello.* London, 1966.

Caesar, Ann. *Characters and Authors in Luigi Pirandello.* New York, 1998.

Cambon, Glauco (ed.). *Pirandello: A Collection of Critical Essays.* Englewood Cliffs, 1967.

Caputi, Anthony. *Pirandello and the Crisis of Modern Consciousness.* Urbana, 1988.

DiGaetani, John L. (ed.). *A Companion to Pirandello Studies.* New York, 1991.

Matthaei, Renate. *Luigi Pirandello.* New York, 1973.

McClintock, Lander. *The Age of Pirandello.* Bloomington, 1951.

Oliver, Roger W. *Dreams of Passion: The Theatre of Luigi Pirandello.* New York, 1979.

Palmer, John. *Studies on the Contemporary Theatre,* London, 1927.

Ragusa, Olga. *Luigi Pirandello.* New York, 1968.

Starkie, Walter. *Luigi Pirandello 1867–1936.* Third edition, revised and enlarged. Berkeley and Los Angeles, 1965.

Vittorini, Domenico. *The Drama of Luigi Pirandello.* Philadelphia, 1935.

CARL R. MUELLER has since 1967 been a professor of theater at UCLA where he has taught in the areas of theater history, criticism, and playwriting. He has won the Samuel Goldwyn Award for Dramatic Writing, and in 1960–61 was a Fulbright Scholar in Berlin. A translator for over forty years, he has translated and published works by Büchner, Brecht, Wedekind, Hauptmann, and Zuckmayer, among others. For Smith and Kraus he has published *Arthur Schnitzler: Four Major Plays, Frank Wedekind: Four Major Plays,* and *August Strindberg: Five Major Plays.* Forthcoming are *Sophokles: The Complete Plays* and *Kleist: Three Major Plays.* His translations have been produced in every part of the English-speaking world.